The Meaning of Life and Faith

Applying the Gospel to Your Life

Bruno Cameron

Contents

Published in Hampton, VA, by Fruition Publishing Concierge Services ®. Fruition Publishing Concierge Services ® is a division of Alesha Brown, LLC.

Fruition Publishing Concierge Services ® can bring authors to your live event. For more information or to book an event, visit Fruition Publishing Concierge Services ® at:

www.FruitionPublishing.com

ISBN: 978-1-954486-67-6 eBook

ISBN: 978-1-954486-68-3 paperback

Library Of Congress Control Number: 2025919696

Introduction

One of the most significant weaknesses for most Christians is truly believing in God the Father, God *the Jesus*, and God the Holy Spirit. We say we do, but how much do we really believe?

People may fully believe in God in one aspect but completely overlook Him in another. When we do that, we are not operating in the fullness of faith nor experiencing the magnitude of His kingship. We were made to depend on God for all our needs and desires. If we don't know who He truly is and how to come into His presence, we are missing out on what God offers us. When I first accepted Jesus as my LORD and Savior, I did not know how much I was missing out on and what I could do if I truly knew who He was and who I was in Him.

To begin with, I was unsure how to pray or what to do when I prayed. I knew what I wanted, so I prayed for that. As I grew older in my belief and formed a relationship with God, revelations and questions flooded my mind. The closer I drew to God, the more I wanted to know, and my questions grew.

I asked people at my church—pastors and theologians—about these questions, and their answers did not quench my thirst. I had questions like:

- How do I pray?
- What is faith?
- How do I apply it to my life?

These were just a few of many. I decided to go on a personal journey, studying as much as I could. I consulted the source, God, rather than other sources. That was when the flame of my questions started to quench, and I grew in the knowledge of God and closer to God. This book may not answer all your questions, but it should answer some of them and give you something to think about. As you continue to read, you will find my answers to some common questions that weighed on my mind. I hope my understanding and revelation of the Word will strengthen your relationship with the Lord God our Father.

What I'm sharing with you should not be taken as the end-all-be-all because we will never know all there is to know about God on this side of heaven. God is manifold in His being; our limited mental abilities can never wrap our minds around the magnitude of His glory.

I want you to remember this: Whatever is written in the Bible is for us to read and study. We may not readily understand everything in the Bible, but we need to be clear that everything written within is something God wants us to know. It is in our best interest to seek out everything God is telling us in the Bible. To get the maximum benefit that God is giving us for free, you must know how to apply the Bible to your life.

Chapter 1

The Meaning of Life

What is life? The answer usually leads to various statements that don't explain the true meaning of life. What I have noticed throughout my years is that most of the answers given focus on how people live their lives and not what life actually is. In this book, I will try to explain what life and faith are and how you can apply them to your everyday life based on what the Bible says. To do so, I consulted the source of life, God the Father. The references in this book are taken from the New King James Version (NKJV) of the Bible. Feel free to reference other versions of the Bible as you read this book for a clearer understanding.

God is the author of life: He determines when life starts, when it stops, and what it is. Let's start our conversation with Psalm 139:13-16 (NKJV) because it describes our topic eloquently as King David talks about how God knows him.

For You formed my inward parts; You covered me in my mother's womb. I will praise You, for I am fearfully and wonderfully made; Marvelous are Your works, And that my soul knows very well. My name was not hidden from You when I was made in secret, and skillfully wrought in the lowest part of the earth. Your eyes saw my substance, being yet informed. And in Your book they all were written, the days fashion for me, when as yet there were none of them.

How beautifully spoken those words are! You can feel the silk poetry of David's words.

The Bible also says in Jeremiah 1:5 (NASB):

Before I formed you in the womb I knew you; Before you were born I sanctified you; I ordained you a prophet to the nations.

Imagine that: God knew you before you were born. Wow! This means I existed in the spirit realm before I existed in the physical world. God knew I was going to be born before I was even conceived!

According to Genesis 1:27 (NIV):

So God created man in His own image; in the image of God He created him; male and female He created them.

This raises the question: Is God male, female, or both? My answer is that God is male. The Bible consistently uses male pronouns and terms when referring to God. (However, it also uses the term man as a neutral gender term, so when God says *in our own image*, there is no distinction between male and female.)

I would like to bring your attention to something very important. When God said He made man in His own image, He was talking about the spirit man. Remember, God is a Spirit, so it was our spirit man that was made in His image. Our flesh man was made in the image of our earthly father and mother, which is why we resemble our parents.

Being a female does not disqualify a woman from being made in God's image. Women are the female version of men, so we can multiply and fill the Earth as God commanded. For me, a few things about creation jumped out immediately. First, the creation of the universe is all physical. We live in it every day.

This is not to say that you can't make spiritual references using creation.

Some people may try to explain some of it spiritually because they lack answers to certain questions. Second, and most importantly, *man* was a living being without mentioning the word *life*. This tells me that man—male and female—existed (moving around, living) on Earth without life. Life was not mentioned until Genesis 2:7 (NKJV):

> *And the Lord God formed man of the dust of the ground, and breathed into his nostrils the breath of life; and man became a living being.*

So what was man before then? Man was a nice clay sculpture without life, doing what God told them to do. Genesis 1:28 (NKJV):

> *Then God blessed them, and God said to them, "Be fruitful and multiply; fill the earth and subdue it; have dominion over the fish of the sea, over the birds of the air, and over every living thing that moves on the earth."*

Think about it: when life leaves the body, it begins the decaying process of returning to its original state —dirt. Another way I can answer the question is that man did receive life momentarily after he was created. I believe that Genesis 2:7 was supposed to be written right after Genesis 1:27. Then it would read like this, starting with Genesis 1:27:

So God created man in His own image; in the image of God He created him; male and female He created them. And the Lord God formed man of the dust of the ground, and breathed into his nostrils the breath of life; and man became a living being.

This would mean that the scholars who compiled the Bible may have made a mistake in organizing the sequential events that took place during man's creation.

What does this all mean regarding man and what life really is? In the book of John 1:4 (ESV) it says, *In Him was life, and the life was the light of men. In Him* references God having life within Him, the giver of life. Man did not have life until God breathed life into him during the initial creation of man, as mentioned in the scriptures I referred to earlier. Therefore, life is a real part of God that He gave to us at the time of conception.

The Bible speaks about life in Proverbs 18:21 (NKJV):

The Meaning of Life and Faith

Death and life are in the power of the tongue, And those who love it will eat it fruit.

This tells me that life is something completely different from the act of how we live—regardless of whether we are affording the so-called finer things in life—it is something inside of us. This scripture tells me I can speak life or death to my existence. The words I speak greatly influence what I choose to say about my living conditions or my future expectations.

If you want to succeed in life, it only makes sense to believe in your goals and speak positively about them. The more you express your desires for success, the more you will start to believe in them, and the words you speak will travel through the channel of faith and give birth to what you are saying.

I believe that when you utter words, you are giving birth to a form of life through faith breathed into us by God in Genesis 2:7.

Now you may be wondering how this works. Let me clear this up for you. God is a spirit, and those who come to Him or worship Him must worship Him in spirit and in truth. You have to come to Him truthfully in belief.

Since God and the Holy Spirit did not always have a definitive form when God breathed life into us, He gave us a part of Himself in a spirit form called *life*. When we speak, we send out a form of the spirit of God mixed with our human spirit and connect with the heavenly realm to retrieve whatever we spoke in the will of God. The faith part of this is our belief in God that forms the vehicle and the passage by which that which we spoke left the heavenly realm and materialized in the earthly realm.

Keep in mind that if you do not believe there is a God and a spirit world, you will never make the connection or create the passageway for that which you speak. Life is not simply about how others define it, nor is it centered on how big your house is, the type of cars you own, the clothes you wear, or how you wine and dine. These things do not define life, but how you can afford to live. John 6:35 (NKJV) says:

And Jesus said to them, "I am the bread of life. He who comes to Me shall never hunger, and he who believes in Me shall never thirst."

Jesus is saying that he is the actual cause of you having life from the day He breathed into you and became a part of you through His breath. Therefore, for you to sustain your life—not how you are living, but how your spirit man stays alive—you have to feed on His word, which is the Word of God.

Having a godly life or living a righteous life requires constantly speaking the Word of God, which is life to our real self—the spirit man. He is telling us that he, Jesus, is the Word that was spoken by God in the beginning. You can see that what we call life has nothing to do with how we live, but how we choose to use our human spirit in agreement with the Holy Spirit, which was given to us by God the Father.

Remember, having the spirit of God in us does not mean we are gods and can do everything God does. Being made in the image of God does come with a degree of power as the children of God. But the extent to which we can do things is predicated on what God says we can do.

If you are still not convinced, let's look at the scripture John 3:16 (NIV):

For God so loved the world that he gave His only begotten Son, that whoever believes in Him should not perish but have everlasting life.

The Bible is telling you that you, as the person we see in the flesh, have another version described as life—

the human spirit. How do I know this? We hear and see it every day when people die. A funeral or home going service is held, yet the body is put in the ground.

Wait a minute! Didn't Jesus just say that if we believe in Him, we should not perish but have everlasting life? This means that the real you will never die. So what happens after your flesh parts ways with the spirit version of you is something we can talk about another time. According to what most of us know today as death, if we are dead and six feet under, what everlasting life is Jesus talking about?

In Genesis chapter 2, God talked about breathing life into mankind He created. That was when and where the other part of our tri-being was placed inside of us, mixed with the Spirit of God. This part of our being can die spiritually, which is a separation of our spirit from God's Spirit. This explains what God meant in Genesis 2:17 (NKJV) when He said:

But of the tree of the Knowledge of good and evil you shall not eat, for in the day that you eat of it you shall surely die.

Notice that the man and woman did not die in the flesh, which requires a six-foot grave. He was not talking about our flesh but our spirit man. So you can see life is not how you live, but another version of us that resides in the flesh—the real you.

Isaiah 55:11 (NKJV) says:

So shall My word be that goes forth from My mouth; It shall not return to Me void, But it shall accomplish what I please, And it shall prosper in the things for which I sent it.

This scripture tells us that when God speaks His Word, the *Spirit* leaves where God is and goes to do what He said. Just as it was in the beginning when God said *Let there be light,* the Word went out of His mouth, created light along with all the other things that were created by God.

Jesus said this in John 6:63 (NKJV):

It is the Spirit who gives life; the flesh profits nothing. The words that I speak to you are spirit, and they are life.

This means that it is not Jesus nor God who gives life, but a result of the triune nature of all three in one.

Now that we understand life from a biblical point of view, let's look at life from a biological point of view. In my limited medical background, a new life starts when a woman's egg and a man's sperm develop in the body at puberty. Notice I said life and not a person because you are not yet a person, but a living organism at that early stage. You become a person when the egg and the sperm become one—that's when you become an individual with a spirit.

Keep in mind, if we were created in God's image, then we are like Him, having three parts to our being —a soul, spirit, and body. I also want you to know that when God made us in His image, He was talking about the spirit, not the flesh. The flesh is created in the image of your parents. So the next time someone asks you what life is, you can answer from a more informed point of view.

Chapter 2

How to Apply Faith

I have given you a reasonable, different perspective on what life is and is not. You can now draw your own conclusion. Let's talk about faith and how we can apply it to our everyday lives. God has created a system or *law* that requires you to believe in Him and do something about what you believe, which provides the pathway for things in the spiritual realm to manifest in the earthly realm. This is the beginning of understanding faith.

The spiritual realm is invisible to us, but it is real. Likewise, many things in the physical world cannot be seen but are real. You don't need to see body aches or pain, nor do you need to see the wind to know that they are there. We have been given five senses to operate effectively in the earthly realm.

To have a better understanding of how faith works, we must define what faith is. Faith is the lifeline between heaven and Earth, or the principle that God put in place for us to keep a close connection with Him. This would include praising Him, worshiping Him, knowing Him, and, most importantly, forming a relationship with Him.

The biblical definition of what faith is, says in Hebrews 11:1 (NKJV), *Now faith is the substance of things hoped for and the evidence of things not seen.* This statement immediately tells us what faith is—it is the substance of something not seen or perceived by the five senses. Since we are dealing with God, the things not seen are a good indication that we are dealing with the spiritual world. What does this all mean? Let us break it down together.

What is a substance? A substance[1] can be a physical material from which something is made or has a discrete existence, neither physical nor tangible. Substances are not always perceived through the five senses. For example, if you are playing soccer, you do not always see the physical ball moving in the open

---

1. Merriam-Webster. (n.d.). *Substance.* In *Merriam-Webster.com dictionary*. Retrieved May 8, 2024, from https://www.merriam-webster.com/dictionary/substance

space, but you position yourself in that space to receive it before the ball is played. This anticipation is based on your understanding of the game, allowing you to see the play before it happens.

What is evidence? *Evidence*[2] can be defined in two ways: first, as an outward sign or indication, and second, as something that furnishes proof, such as a testimony. This means that the actual thing does not have to be within reach or in your immediate line of sight for you to know it exists. The fossils of dinosaurs provide evidence that they once roamed the Earth.

What is hope? Hope[3] is the desire for something to happen, combined with expectation or anticipation that it will. It involves waiting for something to manifest or become true. Hope always looks toward the future and serves as the motivator for our faith. There is something about hope I want to point out, and that is how people use it.

----

2.   Merriam-Webster. (n.d.). *Evidence*. In *Merriam-Webster.com dictionary*. Retrieved May 8, 2024, from https://www.merriam-webster.com/dictionary/evidence.
3.   Merriam-Webster. (n.d.). *Hope*. In *Merriam-Webster.com dictionary*. Retrieved May 8, 2024, from https://www.merriam-webster.com/dictionary/hope.

It is a good thing to have hope as long as you don't end there. Many people get stuck in hope and never move to faith. I have heard people say for years they are hoping for this or that and are still waiting for it to happen. One reason they are not getting the things they are hoping for is that they never put action to their faith, hence failing to enter into faith. So I say to you: don't just live in hope, live by faith.

Things not seen suggest that there are things in question that cannot be seen with the naked eye and are still waiting. Not all things that are unseen are invisible. For example, you might be waiting for someone to join a meeting. Although they are not physically present, they are simply not in your sight. Once they arrive, they are. To put faith into perspective, faith is the act of believing in the existence of something—whether it exists in the spiritual or earthly realm—even when you do not physically possess it.

If what you are hoping for is in the earthly realm, all you need to do is believe you can have it. See it in your mind as yours—as long as it is in the will of God for your life—and perform the actions to receive it. You should start acting or preparing for it as if you have received what you are hoping for. Put in the earthly work that makes you qualify for what you desire. This could be a job, depending on where you are in life, or you might need to study for a test, fill out applications, or network to obtain what you desire.

Let's say you want something not of a physical nature (something in the spiritual realm). You first have to believe that there is a God who lives in the heavenly realm, and He is a rewarder of those who diligently seek to do His will, and all other things will be added unto them.

The Bible also tells us how to use faith. Romans 4:17 (NKJV) says:

> *God, who gives life to the dead and calls those things which do not exist as though they did.*

By doing this, you are declaring that God exists and that He gives you things. Some people may say that if you do that, you are telling a lie. I beg to differ. It would be a lie if you were calling something that does not exist as though it does for the purpose of deception, evilness, or something outside of God's will. But if you are calling something that does not exist as though it does with the expectation and hope

25

of something good, then all you are doing is exercising the principle of faith.

As long as you believe God can do it, and it's already done, you automatically create a connection for what God has for you. When you receive it will depend on the level of your faith, which is the corresponding work or action you put in. As long as you don't waver in your faith, you will receive. James 2:14-17 (NKJV) also says:

What does it profit, my brethren, if someone says he has faith but does not have works? Can faith save him?

These two scriptures tell you that believing is not enough to receive what you hope for. You are not exercising faith just because you believe in something. Think about this for a minute: You are standing on the diving board at a swimming pool in your local recreation center, and with a loud voice, you get everyone's attention. You say very boldly and with the confidence of a gold medalist: *I can make the most perfect dive from this platform.* Your statement can be as sure as getting your finger wet if you dip it in water. That perfect dive will never come to pass until your belief aligns with your action of diving from the diving board. You will stand there until the sun stops shining, otherwise.

What if I told you that the devil and his demons believe there is a God? James 2:19 (NKJV) says:

You believe that there is one God. You do well. Even the demons believe—and tremble!

Just believing won't help you. What James is saying is that demons believe there is a God, but they don't have faith in Him. Don't be that guy.

Here is an important question you might be asking: *If something is invisible, how do I know it's there to hope for it?* The simple answer is everything that is in the will of God that you can imagine exists in the spiritual world. God provides for us, and His people shall not be left begging for bread or in want. God said in Psalm 23 that if we make Him our Shepard, we shall not want. So if you are in want, you should ask yourself if you have made the Lord your Shepard.

He also tells us that the spirit man has a divine connection with the Holy Spirit, a connection that was made right from the start when life was given to man after he was formed from the dust of the earth. With this in mind, we can better understand what faith is.

According to Hebrews 11:1, faith involves the act of waiting, longing, or expecting something that is not seen or cannot be seen in the earthly realm, yet we know it exists in the spiritual realm. Once you speak God's word, which is the Holy Spirit, the Holy Spirit sends angels to fulfill what you said. James 2:26 reminds us that Jesus came to give us life and life more abundantly, so we should not be lacking anything we want or need.

Another way to explain this concept is to use the radio station analogy. Think of the spiritual realm like a radio station constantly emitting radio frequencies. Even when your radio is turned off, it is transmitting a frequency. As soon as you turn on your radio and tune into a specific signal, you will receive whatever is being broadcast. That is the same way God's blessings are—His station always transmits blessings specifically for you to receive. When you activate your faith, you turn on your faith radio and tune into His frequency, where you can receive those blessings.

This also means that God is not going to start providing for you after you tune in. He has already transmitted and made provision for whatever you are asking for as long as it is in His will. People say that they are just waiting for God to do this or that in their lives when, in fact, they need to put their faith to work and tune their faith radio to God's frequency.

I want to point out another thing people say that makes no sense and does not align with belief, but weakens their faith, and most don't even realize it. Christians believe that God is everywhere, which is true, depending on the context.

"He may not show up when you want Him to, but He is always on time."

If He is everywhere, exactly where is He coming from to show up on time? We need to stop repeating these foolish sayings.

God our Father tells us that everything we need is already provided; we only need to receive it. The first time He told us this was during the creation of the universe. Being an all-knowing God, He knew all we would need and want. When He created the world, He provided all we will ever need because He is God and knows everything. He is omniscient.

1 John 3:20 (NKJV) tells us:

For if our heart condemns us, God is greater than our heart, and knows all things.

How do I know this? God told us in Genesis 1 in the creation story. Notice what He said after He created the things of this world. *And God saw that it was good.* Think about it—aerodynamics, gravity, and all the other laws of physics were not made when these well-known physicists understood how they worked and how to use them. It was already in existence long before they knew about those laws. He told us this again in Matthew 6:8 (NKJV) when He said:

Therefore do not be like them. For the Father knows the things you have need of before you ask Him.

Knowing this, we should have the boldness and confidence to ask for whatever we desire in His will, knowing we will receive it.

A mistake that some people make with faith is thinking that some don't have faith. They will say something like, *I don't have any faith.* While that's not true, everyone has a different measure of faith. We have earthly faith like when we jump in a taxi and ask the driver to take us to our destination. We have faith that the taxi driver will take us to our destination, and most do not question it. The same should go for God. Romans 12:3 (NKJV) says:

For I say, through the grace given to me, to everyone

who is among you, not to think of himself more highly than he ought to think, but to think soberly, as God has dealt to each one a measure of faith.

There are a lot of things going on in the spirit realm that we are not aware of, that are trying to take us out every chance they get. To think we do not need the blessings or grace of God is to think more highly than we should.

The KJV of the Bible says it better:

God has dealt to each one the measure of faith.

Saying *a measure of faith* versus *the measure of faith* implies that there is a difference in people's faith levels. No one person has more faith than the other. It may not seem like this when you look at others' achievements, prosperity, and lives. Some people seem to have everything going well for them. This cannot be further from the truth than the east is from the west. The fact is, they exercise their faith more than others.

Think of it like this: God has dealt to every man the measure of time. We all have the same 24 hours in a day, but some people complain that the day is too short, while some seem to have all the time in the world. Why is that? Some people manage their time wisely, and some don't. The same is true when it comes to faith. It all comes down to how you use it and how often.

How do you get faith? Let's start with Romans 10:17 (NKJV):

So then faith comes by hearing, and hearing by the word of God.

Just as long as your actions correspond with the Word of God, that is faith in itself. You are acting on someone's word that you only have evidence of. What if I told you that hearing other words that are not God's can still lead to faith? Yes, you heard correctly. Your boss tells you he will pay you after you work for him. You do the work and he pays you regularly. Your action of working with the belief that you will get paid as promised is you having faith in your boss or employer.

Romans 10:17 emphasizes that hearing and words are involved in developing faith. This verse highlights the importance of listening to spoken words, specifically *the word of God*, but doesn't say who we must listen to in order to hear His word. You can hear it from your pastor, a church leader, or yourself.

If you hear it from yourself, you need to read the Bible aloud.

Romans 10:17 gives a principle about faith—how God designed it to work. As a principle, it can be used for the wrong reason and still produce results. If you plant corn, corn is what will sprout from the ground, not tomatoes.

The ground does not determine what grows, but the seed does. Based on what you want, determine what seed of faith you plant. If you want prosperity in your life, plant the seed that produces that (every seed produces after its own kind). Hearing the prosperity word of God will grow prosperity in your life. How do you hear from God or know what you're hearing is from God? It's easier than you think.

When you read the Bible, you are actually listening and hearing the words of God. Remember that not every word in the Bible is God's spoken word. You must pray to God to help you rightly divide and discern His word. This may be an eye-opener for some, but the Bible has lies in it—other people's opinions and even the devil's words. When the serpent told Eve that she would not die if she ate from the tree of the knowledge of good and evil, that was a lie.

In 1 Corinthians 7:25-40, when Paul speaks on the unmarried and widows about the dos and don'ts, that was His view on the topic. As you can see, it takes careful study of the Bible to know which words belong to God and how to rightly divide the truth. Just because not all of the Bible was spoken by God or His prophets, disciples, apostles, and teachers does not mean it wasn't inspired by Him. There is a big difference between inspirationally written and the inspired word of God.

The Bible also tells you that faith without works is dead. James 2:20 (NKJV) says:

But do you want to know, O foolish man, that faith without works is dead?

What James is saying is that in order to get what you are seeking in faith, you have to do something. Believing alone won't make what you have faith in God for become a reality. It requires some work on your part.

Remember the woman in the Bible with the issue of blood? Before she left her home, she believed Jesus could heal her to the point that she thought if she could only touch the hem of His garment, *she would be made whole*. Although her faith was great, she had to take action and put forth some work. The work she put in was at the risk of getting stoned if she was seen in public during the time of her menstrual cycle.

The other part of her work was pressing through the crowd and not giving up, regardless of how large the crowd was. It was not until she put in the work of leaving her home and pressing through the crowd to touch the hem of his garment that Jesus healed her.

Chapter 3

Praying For Results

L iving a Christian life cannot be done without praying. That's just how God designed it. This process is also a form of worship and praise.

Praying is probably the one true way we know how to exercise and express our faith in God personally. In other words, praying is a true outward and inward manifestation of believing in God. Why do I say that? Because when you pray, you are actually having a conversation with someone unseen who hears and will answer you.

We talk to people almost every day, and we don't have to guess if they hear us. If the conversation is on the phone, we hear an audible response, confirming they heard us.

Whenever you pray, you should always try to keep it audible and not silent, as many do. Silent prayers do not bring faith because there is no hearing taking place, and if there is no faith, God is not pleased. Hebrews 11:6 (NKJV) says:

But without faith it is impossible to please Him, for he who comes to God must believe that He is, and that He is a rewarder of those who diligently seek Him.

If you are trying to please Him, you must do it His way—in true faith and not your way or however you feel like doing it. What is true faith versus untrue faith? Faith that is not true can be a person pretending they believe something when they do not.

For example, if believing was a location and you pray to God to meet you up north, where you pretend to be, but you are actually down south. You would miss Him because God is not going to meet you where you are pretending to be in faith, but where you are. Plus, if He shows up where you pretend to be, you won't be there to receive what you ask for.

Do you remember the man who brought his son to Jesus' disciples for them to heal him and they could not, so he asked Jesus to heal his son? Mark 9:24 (NKJV):

Immediately, the father of the child cried out and said with tears, "Lord, I believe; help my unbelief!"

Did you notice that the man did not pretend to fully believe Jesus could heal his son? This was probably because of the failed attempt of the disciples. The most important thing is that he did not pretend to be fully in faith. He immediately asked Jesus to help his unbelief. Don't try to trick God. Be honest with where you are in your faith.

John 4:24 tells us that *God is Spirit, and those who worship Him must worship in spirit and truth.* Since God is a spirit, when we worship Him, it must be on a spiritual level. (Remember, there are prayers of worship.) Knowing all that, let me put this into perspective for you.

Hebrews 11:1 (KJV) says:

Now faith is the substance of things hoped for, the evidence of things not seen.

Romans 10:17 (NKJV) says:

So then faith comes by hearing, and hearing by the word of God.

This means you can't hear unless there is *talking*, not *thinking*. If you are going to have faith, it needs to be uttered. Mark 11:23 (NKJV) sums it up for us:

For assuredly, I say to you, whoever says to this mountain, 'Be removed and be cast into the sea,' and does not doubt in his heart, but believes that those things he says will be done, he will have whatever he says.

Notice that Jesus tells us three times in this one verse to *say*. He never once told us to *think* about what we want to happen or are praying for.

Let me focus your attention on something that you may not know and need to know. When you pray, your prayer is not a command for God to do anything. You can't make God do anything that is not in His will. God does not move just because we pray. Our whaling and shouting do not make God move to our demands. Don't put God in a box! The Bible talks about God working in John 5:19-20.

What's the purpose of praying? I believe one of God's biggest desires is for us to have a relationship with

Him. Notice I said a relationship with Him and not the other way around—He already has one with us. Praying maintains and increases our relationship with God the Father, and fasting does the same. That is why the sole purpose of speaking in a heavenly language is to enhance our prayer life and is partially the reason Paul said to pray without ceasing.

What I'm about to say may come as a surprise to some, but study the Word of God and ask Him to reveal to you the purpose of praying. If you diligently seek His answer, you will know that the sole purpose of praying is not to ask God for things of this world for personal gain or to indulge in. The Bible says to:

Seek first the kingdom of God and His righteousness, and all these things shall be added to you (Matthew 6:33, NKJV).

If you want to know what things God is talking about, go to verse 25 and read back down to verse 33. If we do as He says, then we do not need to ask for material things.

Many people will tell you they heard God's audible voice. In reality, it was the Holy Spirit within them speaking so loudly that it seemed like an audible voice. Ever noticed that most making this claim can't tell you what the voice sounds like, only how sure they are it was God's voice? God sounds like us when He speaks through the Holy Spirit. In the Old and early New Testament days, people would hear God's voice audibly. People today use those scriptures to justify their beliefs or try to convince people that they hear God's voice. Is God not speaking to us audibly anymore?

Before Jesus went back to heaven, he said he would send us the Holy Spirit to comfort us and he would live inside us, bringing things to our remembrance. Since God lives inside us, there would be no reason for Him to speak to us in an audible voice from heaven.

In the Old Testament days, the Holy Spirit was not working in that capacity because Jesus had not yet fulfilled the law. The problem is that most people don't listen to the voice of God inside them. They associate God's voice with their mind, instinct, or feelings.

Remember, many of the things God did and did through Jesus in biblical times were unique to prepare for Jesus' arrival, and Jesus did what He did to fulfill the prophecy and represent God in the flesh. This will not happen again since Jesus has come and gone while we wait for His second coming.

One of the biggest parts of praying is speaking, and words are required unless you speak with your hands (sign language). To show you how important words are, God used words to create the universe. Isaiah 55:11 (NKJV) says:

So shall My word be that goes forth from My mouth; It shall not return to Me void, But it shall accomplish what I please, And it shall prosper in the thing for which I sent it.

The main reason Jesus did all He did when He was walking in the flesh is proven in John 14:10 and John 5:19.

Meditate on that for a while and think about the fact that we were given that kind of power. I wonder how it works for people who are mute. It is mind-boggling how people would trick themselves into believing they heard God's voice when they can't even *hear* the things that He has already said in the Bible.

Speaking about hearing the audible voice of God, how would you know if you heard it? You would have to look at the track record of how and when He spoke in the past. Now remember Malachi 3:6 says *He is the same yesterday and forever,* and He is to be because if He is not, we would all be confused and He would be untrustworthy.

The Bible only mentions God speaking directly from heaven four times, three of which He was either speaking to Jesus or about Jesus. The other time, He was speaking to Paul. When Paul heard God's voice from heaven, it came with a commanding factor of wanting to bow down and worship out of reverence, and a fear of reverence came over them.

If your experience was not something like those mentioned, you might want to reevaluate your experience hearing the voice of God. The Bible says the voice of God sounds like thunder, many waters, like harps (read Exodus 19:19, Job 37:4-5, Psalm 29:3, Revelation 4:1 and 14:2). The Bible also says God's voice sometimes sounds even like us (1 Samuel 3:4-10 and Revelation 1:12). I mention all that to say that in a meaningful conversation, one person speaks while the other listens. When it's God's time to talk —audibly or through His written Word (the Bible) —it's important to know who is speaking.

What I take from Isaiah 55:11 is that when God speaks, it is not idle words, nor does He speak as some of us do. This also means that when God speaks, things happen. He does not speak just because He can.

Since we are talking about praying, which requires words, I think it's best to pray His words over our situation so we can get what we are praying for. This also tells me that the best way to pray is to find out what God says about your needs and incorporate His words in your prayer rather than just yours. This is not to say that you should not pray your own words. I'm simply saying His words carry more weight than ours, and angels react to His words.

When we pray, we should be careful of the things we say because our words have life, and we should utter them with expectancy rather than carelessly. Angels only move by the word of God. Psalm 103:20a (NKJV) says:

> *Bless the Lord, you His angels, who excel in strength, who do His word, heeding the voice of His word.*

Notice the verse says that angels heed the voice of His words and not His voice. So that means whoever echoes God's words will cause God's angels to move on His words on behalf of their needs. If you are not praying God's word or His will, no matter how sincere you are, you could be praying amiss. James 4:3 (NKJV) tells us this:

You ask and do not receive, because you ask amiss, that you may spend it on your pleasure.

This scripture is simply saying you can ask for something in the wrong manner or for the wrong reason.

The same way we conduct ourselves appropriately when we talk to people in authority is the same way we need to talk to God. Praying is not just talking to God, as some say. Praying needs to be taught, which is why the disciples asked Jesus to teach them how to pray (the only thing they ever asked Jesus to teach them). This means that if you haven't been taught how to pray, you will not be able to do it correctly.

If someone prays incorrectly, they might end up getting their prayer answered by the devil or inadvertently answer their own prayer. How? It happens when you want something so badly that you listen to your feelings and thoughts rather than waiting for God's answer and direction. You might be hoping for a specific answer from God and trying to shape the outcome to fit your wishes. This is how you end up answering your own prayer.

Remember the story of Abram and his wife Sarai when God told Abram they would have a child? At first, they laughed at the idea because they were old, but after a while, their faith grew in God's word. Between the time God made Abram the promise and when the promised child was born was about twenty years. Sarai took it upon herself to help God by giving Abram permission to sleep with her maidservant (Genesis 16:1-4).

The other thing is people don't believe that the devil is listening to our prayers and will give them things, including answers to prayers, especially if it fits his motive operandi of them destroying themselves unknowingly when they pray wrongly. Daniel 10:12-13 (NKJV) says:

Then he said to me, "Do not fear, Daniel, for from the first day that you set your heart to understand, and to humble yourself before your God, your words were heard; and I have come because of your words. But the prince of the kingdom of Persia withstood me twenty-one days; and behold, Michael, one of the chief princes, came to help me, for I had been left alone there with the kings of Persia."

This tells us that there is a heavenly war going on because the devil hears our prayers and works to prevent us from receiving the answers from God.

There is also a battle of the mind, which stems from seeds the devil planted in their mind years ago. The devil can't be everywhere at the same time, so to influence people all over the world, he plants seeds that germinate later in their lives.

The devil can harm you in many ways, one of which is answering a prayer that was prayed wrongly or from a person who is impatiently waiting for their faith to connect with the will of God. With them unaware that they prayed wrongly, receiving something that seemed to be right on time when it really was the devil. In the end, this is how some people leave believing that God did them wrong. Job 1:6-7 (NKJV) says:

Now there was a day when the sons of God came to present themselves before the LORD, and Satan also came among them. And the Lord said to Satan, "From where do you come?" So Satan answered the Lord and said, "From going to and fro on the earth, and from walking back and forth on it."

What does this tell you? Satan, our enemy, is listening to our conversation, seeking to destroy us through our fellowship with God our Father. If he could know that there was a meeting going on with God and His sons, why is it hard for you to believe that he knows your plans when you speak them aloud? When Satan hears us praying wrongly and not the word of God or His will, he seeks the opportunity to steal, kill, or destroy us.

In the above scripture, did you realize that the devil spoke the truth when God spoke to him? Just because he is the father of lies doesn't mean he can't be honest. He will do it if he thinks it will benefit him.

The devil cannot harm you until you open your mouth and start bragging about what you are going to do or share your plans with someone who is not on one accord with you. The devil does not have the power to know what you are thinking, but when you talk and pray, you should be careful of the things you say. You should never use harmful words, even if you think it's funny or you don't mean what you are saying. The devil will use those words later in your life or against the person you spoke them over, to hurt you or them. Isaiah 54:17 (NKJV) says:

No weapon formed against you shall prosper, And every tongue which rises against you in judgment You shall condemn. This is the heritage of the servants of the LORD, And their righteousness is from Me," Says the LORD.

Let's say you are praying to God for $10. While you are praying to God, the devil shows up and intercepts your prayer because you prayed incorrectly or with no faith. Because you did not pray correctly, you tied the hands of God. God allows your situation to play out, even though He knows that's not the best thing for you. When you pray outside of God's principles, there is nothing He can do because He would have to go back on His word, and that would be a lie. God cannot lie.

In this scenario, God wanted to give you a job instead, so God sent out His angels to get the process rolling based on your level of faith. Before the process was complete, instead of you getting a job, the devil gave you the $10. You thought that was the best thing for you, but you did not have enough faith to believe in God for what He wanted to give you. A job is far better than receiving $10. You will need money again in the next day or so. The devil gave you that $10 to keep you in need, which can lead to bigger problems later. Remember what the Bible said in Romans 8:26-27 (NKJV):

Likewise, the Spirit also helps in our weaknesses. For we

do not know what we should pray for as we ought, but the Spirit Himself makes intercession for us with groaning which cannot be uttered. Now He who searches the heart knows what the mind of the Spirit is, because He makes intercession for the saints according to the will of God.

Before translation, in the original scripture, we groan, not the Holy Spirit. The Holy Spirit intercedes regarding our groaning when we do not know how to pray for our needs. Therefore, we can pray incorrectly when we don't know what or how to pray. This allows the devil to sneak in and answer our prayer, putting us deeper in trouble or need. When things go wrong, we often ask why God let this or that happen to us, when we are the ones who did not pray the right way or for the right things.

If praying is a conversation with God, then one person should be listening while the other is talking. God listens when we pray, but are we listening when He talks? One of our weaknesses is that we are not always in faith when we pray, nor are we always praying in God's will or praying correctly in faith. Sometimes, we don't take the time to listen to God's reply or wait for His response.

I often hear people say that maybe God wants them to do this or that, or is telling them this or that. Those same people are the ones who claim to have a message from God for you. If they are so sure God gave them a word for you, then why are they not sure about the word from God for their lives? Just a thought.

Now that we know more about praying, the next thing is to know how to pray properly. Let's look at how a conversation would go if you were talking to your earthly father. You would address him appropriately. You would not be shouting at him or calling his name after every three words. Many people think that they have to take a certain position when they pray for God to hear them—not true.

As I said before, praying does not make God do anything, although praying is involved in making things happen. So the next time you pray, ask yourself: Is my action relevant to the prayer for it to be answered? Some people think wearing a prayer shawl, counting a string of beads, closing their eyes, jumping up and down, or changing the tone of their voice (screaming at the top of their lungs) is necessary for prayer.

No one has meaningful conversations with anyone on earth that way. Does God answer prayers because we do these things, or has He already provided what we need? If we believe that is true, why do we treat God in those ridiculous ways? I have noticed that the prayers that God answered swiftly for me are the ones that were short and to the point when I was in a state of calm, doing something totally unrelated to my petition, while I was praying.

Another thing that people believe when it comes to prayer is that God will answer a clergy's prayer quicker than theirs. Remember, praying is not a negotiation with God to do something—you are not trying to convince or trick Him into doing what you want or how you want it to be done. Whatever you pray for is done long before you ask for it. The Bible says the Father knows the things you have need of before you ask Him (Matthew 6:5-8). When God saw that His creation was good, He declared that nothing further was required for our needs.

Maybe you need to remind yourself who you are talking to. Do you talk to your earthly father or anybody like that? No, so why would you treat God like that? His Spirit is within us, so all the dramatics are unnecessary, and it proves you are praying because of your works, and not from a point of faith.

More importantly, when we pray, we should stay in faith and not plead that God does this or that for us.

The minute we say please, we are not in faith. We are now praying in fear, fearing God will not do what we are asking Him for, or He has not done what He said He has done. Saying the word please in a prayer denotes no trust in God, and you are unstable in your faith. 1 John 5: 14-15 (NKJV):

Now this is the confidence that we have in Him, that if we ask anything according to His will, He hears us. And if we know that He hears us, whatever we ask, we know that we have the petitions that we asked of Him.

This also means that if we are in faith, we only need to pray for something once, according to His will. The next time we mention it to God, we should thank Him for whatever we asked for until it comes to fruition.

Remember Daniel 10:12-13? The angel said that he was on his way to deliver what Daniel asked for, but was intercepted by the devil, trying to prevent Daniel from getting the answer to his prayer. In the first part of that verse, the angel told Daniel, *Do not fear*. The angel was letting Daniel know he should not let delay cause him to doubt, which could cause him to beg. For us, that would be saying, *please-God-please*, which would be praying in fear.

Another thing we must know about prayer is that there are different types, such as prayers of petition, prayers of thanksgiving, and prayers of worship. Since there are different prayers, there are different rules. The same way you would not use the rules of football to play a basketball game, the same goes for praying. Too often, people will pray a prayer of petition the same way they pray a prayer of thanksgiving. You will always be out of faith if you do that.

What does the Bible say about praying? Psalm 100:4 (NKJV) says:

> *Enter into His gates with thanksgiving, and into His courts with praise. Be thankful to Him, and bless His name.*

What does this all mean? If you had the chance to speak to the King of England or the President of the United States, you wouldn't be able to walk through the gate and demand what you want. You could not yell in their face, repeating their names a thousand times in the conversation, expecting them to take us seriously. I guarantee they would throw you out if you approached or spoke to them in that manner.

God is due even more respect than we give those figures of authority. We must show Him reverence, be thankful, and bless His name. Be bold but humble and glorify God for who He is and what He has done for us. The Psalmist tells us to come into God's courts and into His gates, meaning that you should take a posture of reverence and have a mindset of total devotion towards God.

The other thing you must remember is to seek first the kingdom of God, and all other things will be added. Matthew 6:25-34 instructs us not to worry about the basic needs of life like money, food, clothes, and where to live. If we spend our time praying for those things or are not satisfied with what or where we are in life, then we may need to ask ourselves if we are seeking God's kingdom first.

Most importantly, whenever you ask for something, you must ask in the name of Jesus Christ. *And whatever you ask in My name, that I will do, that the Father may be glorified in the Son* (John 14:13, NKJV).

Let's look at the prayer template closely to see what Jesus is saying. Let's meditate on what Jesus is saying when He said *whatever*. Is Jesus telling us that regardless of what you want or need, you can ask God for it in His name? If you do that, you would be using the LORD's name in vain, and God would not approve. Like I said earlier, if you are asking for something that is outside the will of God, then your walk with God will be in question.

Do you ever wonder what it really means when we say *in Jesus' name* at the end of our prayer? We are asking God to hear us through the blood of Jesus and to respond to us as if Jesus were the one talking to Him. It also means we are using the authority of Jesus Christ.

Also, when you pray, don't use mindless repetition or be ostentatious before men, but be fervent when praying to God because He knows what you need before you ask. God wants us to ask properly, as He told us in the Bible, which would mean lining up our faith with what He has already provided and given to us. Matthew 6:5-8 says:

When you pray it should not be to draw attention to yourself, this is not to say that every time you pray you have to be in your closet or in private. When you pray it should be honest, sincere in faith and should be in the Father's will and the Father's will only.

There are people who pray to Jesus, asking Him to give them things or do something for them. But should we be praying to Jesus or God? Jesus told us who we should pray to in the prayer template he provided in Matthew 6:9-13 (NKJV):

Jesus said, Our Father in heaven, Hallowed be Your name. Your kingdom come. Your will be done On earth as it is in heaven. Give us this day our daily bread. And forgive us our debts, As we forgive our debtors. And do not lead us into temptation, But deliver us from the evil one. For Yours is the kingdom and the power and the glory forever.

First, this is not the LORD's prayer or a prayer. Jesus was giving his disciples a manner to model their prayer when they prayed. Also, remember this manner of praying was before the Holy Spirit had come, meaning they were praying under the law, so you should not be praying that way now. Mark 11:25-26 (NKJV) says:

And whenever you stand praying, if you have anything against anyone, forgive him, that your Father in heaven may also forgive you your trespasses. But if you do not forgive, neither will your Father in heaven forgive your trespasses.

Under the law, that is exactly what you should do because they were not under grace yet.

This means that you must first forgive, which is of your works, before God can forgive you and hear your prayer (read 1 Kings 8:31-36). That is how it was under the law (not so now). You notice they had to forgive before God would answer their prayer, just like in Abraham's time. Neither Jesus nor His disciples ever prayed those exact words as a prayer.

Notice what Jesus did first in the model prayer. He included himself as a child of God, not exempting himself from doing it either. *Our Father in heaven* would mean that if you were to pray to Jesus the Son, you would be praying to the wrong person. All prayers go through Jesus, not to the Son. Jesus then acknowledged the holiness of God's name and that it should be treated as such, which still applies today.

The next verse lets us know that we should pray for God's kingdom to come and His will to be done on earth, not our will. The kingdom Jesus is talking about is the Holy Spirit. Remember, Jesus said he would send the Helper and that the kingdom is within us. One of the biggest things that jumped out at me from that statement was that God is not in control of everything going on in the earthly realm, contrary to what most people believe. Therefore, everything that is happening on earth is not the will of God. You could also look at it as God's will is already settled and complete in heaven, and we should pray for the same. So whose will is being done? The devil's and ours!

People often say God is sovereign over everything that is going on in the world. If that were true, why would Jesus tell us to pray for God's will to be done on earth if it was already being done on earth?

The other thing to note is that God cannot just impose His will on earth as He sees fit, which is why Jesus told us to pray for God's will to be done on earth. What I want you to take away from this is that, despite how powerful God is and has the ability to do anything, He prioritizes His integrity over His ability. That should show you how much of a God He is.

Is God's will being done on earth as it is in heaven? No. I don't believe there are any diseases, murders, wars, or any form of injustice taking place in heaven. One reason why Jesus told us to pray for God's will to be done on earth is that the earth's systems should mirror heaven's systems, and they do not.

Jesus let us know that we should feed on God's words the same way we feed our fleshly bodies daily with food. This reminds me of when God fed the Israelites in the wilderness with manna. It was a daily feeding, which they were forbidden, and they could not take more than a one-day supply. Even though they were being fed with physical food, in Matthew 6:11, Jesus is referring to physical and spiritual food. He told the devil about the spiritual food when He was being tempted.

The Bible tells us that God's words are life, and we must partake of them daily if we want life. The next verse is the verse most of us struggle with, and some don't think about what they are saying when they repeat it. If we knew what this verse meant, some of us wouldn't be asking God to do it to us.

Forgive us our trespasses as we forgive those who trespass against us.

Do we really want God to forgive us our debts as we forgive our debtors? We don't always forgive our debtors and when we do, it comes with conditions and stipulations, or we blackmail them later for offending us. That would be very problematic if we were still living under the law, which is the only time that it applies. Since we are now living under grace, that part of the verse does not apply to us.

Why do I say that? Read Ephesians 4:25-32 and pay particular attention to the word *forgave*, which is in the past tense. This is how grace makes the difference. After Christ sacrificed for us, we no longer needed to forgive others to get God to answer our prayers. Instead, we are forgiven by God, and because He has forgiven us, we should forgive others. Colossians 3:13 drives home the point, and so does 1 John 2:12. Hopefully, these scriptures clear up any confusion.

The next verse is often poorly translated, which can lead people to believe that God is leading them into temptation. This would not make sense. Why would God tempt us just to turn around and deliver us from His temptation? What the scripture is telling us is not to live in such a way that we are led into temptation, but we should seek deliverance from evil. Psalm 23 reminds us that God guides us in the path of righteousness.

So the next time you go to pray, ask yourself, *Am I asking according to God's will, praying how Jesus told me to pray? Am I praying in faith? What does it profit, my brethren, if someone says he has faith but does not have works? Can faith save him* (James 2:14, NKJV)?

It's important to realize that repeating Bible verses doesn't automatically make what you say come true. Believe what you are saying and then back it up with action.

Ever wonder how you get whatever you pray for? Have you ever heard someone say, *God is going to do it for you, and all you have to do is just pray*? I believe you first have to believe there is a God and He can do all things. Second, you have to recognize that there is a spiritual world. God lives in the spiritual world, so a lot of what we are asking for is in a spiritual form or right here on earth.

Everything you will ever need, want, and will benefit God's kingdom is already here on earth or in heaven. If you think that your prayers are telling God what to do, you are sadly mistaken. Our prayer is not a command for God to stop what He is doing and run to our aid, especially if it is not done right. When we pray correctly, what we are actually doing is joining forces with God in carrying out His will on earth or in our lives.

The biggest thing we need to know is that God's kingdom comes first and is what His will is about. Once you know that deep down in your heart, you will understand why we should pray for the betterment of His kingdom. In doing so, the personal stuff we want are just add-ons for seeking first the kingdom. Getting what you want is predicated on putting God's will first and living according to His will. God should be first in our lives, no matter what. Matthew 16:24-25 (NKJV) says the following about putting God first in our lives:

> *Then Jesus said to His disciples, "If anyone desires to come after Me, let him deny himself, and take up his cross, and follow Me. For whoever desires to save his life will lose it, but whoever loses his life for My sake will find it."*

Getting your prayers answered does not depend on your tone of voice, volume, physical location, what you wear, your customs and rituals, or how many times you say *Father God* or *oh God*, in your prayer. If you pray in the manner in which Jesus told His disciples to pray and do it in faith, you will not have to be concerned about your prayers being answered.

Now that you have some more knowledge on how to pray, the next question you might ask is, *Does God answer every prayer, or did He just not hear me when I prayed?* Remember, no response can be the only answer you will get (God does not waste words).

Sometimes, when you don't get what you asked for, it leads to a sea of assumptions about God. As a result, you might reason that it was not for you or wasn't supposed to be, which might be true.

Read Mathew 20:20-28 (NKJV) and you will see what the answer could be. In the scripture, there is a reference to Zebedee's two sons and their mother. The mother asked Jesus to grant her two sons the right and left seats in His kingdom. She asked for something wrong for the taking, but she probably did not know that was wrong, based on Jesus' response:

> *But to sit on My right hand and on My left is not mine to give, but it is for those for whom it is prepared.*

People who pray for personal and selfish motives will not get their prayers answered either. Psalm 66:18 (NKJV) tells us, *If I regard iniquity in my heart, the Lord will not hear.* How much clearer can the Bible be in letting you know that God will not answer all prayers? James 1:8 (NKJV) confirms this:

> *But let him ask in faith, with no doubting, for he who doubts is like a wave of the sea driven and tossed by the wind. For let not that man suppose that he will receive*

anything from the Lord; he is a double-minded man, unstable in all his ways.

Is that enough proof for you?

If you practice praying as discussed earlier, you will get your prayers answered every time. You don't need to ask your pastor to pray for you because you believe their prayer will be answered over yours, although there is nothing wrong with them praying for you or agreeing with you in prayer.

People run straight to Matthew 18:20's reference of *where two or three are gathered in my name I am in the middle*...I want you to notice that the verse did not say *where two or three are praying*, it says *gathered*. Multiple people can pray together, but not be aligned in their thoughts and faith.

At the same time, you should have the confidence that your prayer will be answered just as Pastor So-and-So's. God is not a respecter of persons when it comes to answering prayers because we are all given the same access to Him. Act 10:34-35 (Treasury of Scripture) says:

Then Peter opened his mouth, and said, Of a truth I perceive that God is no respecter of persons; But in every nation he that fears him, and works righteousness, is accepted with him.

Praying for, with, or over someone is always a good thing to do. We should be able to agree on one accord with our brothers and sisters with our prayers. The issue is that if I agree with them without knowing God's will, it may go against His plan.

You cannot intercede for someone about something that they do not believe in God for, no matter how much they lack in their life. It's always best to just ask the Holy Spirit to intercede for someone when you are not sure what they believe or what they want you to pray for. Successful prayer requires understanding God's will and aligning your faith and belief with what you are praying for.

When we talk about prayer, we must remember there's a process for prayer. Why? Mankind's deception resulted in the transfer of world dominion to Satan, which then prevented God from legally acting in the world. God created the system called prayer to have legal access to the world, anytime and anywhere. There is a process that this system must follow for it to work efficiently when we do our part correctly.

Prayer starts with God—it is always about Him and Him only, which means we should ask for His will to be done on Earth (Matthew 6:9-13). This allows God to release His will on the earth through the Holy Spirit.

There are four major parts to the praying process: the Holy Spirit, the Son (Jesus Christ), and us, the believer. God set the standard by His words in the first step of the process. Read 1 Corinthians 2:10, Romans 11:36, and Revelation 4:11. As you can see from those three scriptures, it is all about God.

The Holy Spirit is the second step in the process. He is a helper who helps us with our weaknesses, wisdom, knowledge, and understanding of who God is. You can learn more about this in Romans 8:26-27 and John 14:16-18. As you can see, we need help always, and the Holy Spirit does His part in the process of prayer.

Jesus the Son of God, having all power and authority in heaven and earth, gave us the right to use His name, which lets us know we have the same rights and authority to petition God. This is the third step. He makes intercession for us. He is our mediator and advocate. We need to know that we cannot get to God without going through Him; He is the only way. That is part of the reason why we cannot pray to God without using His name.

Then there is us. We speak the word of God in this world with the kingdom of God in us, giving God the channel to do His will on earth through us. We are a very important part of the prayer process, as you will see from the following scriptures: Ezekiel 22:30, Thessalonians 5:16-19, Ephesians 6:18, and Romans 8:26-27.

Therefore, if the will of God is not being done on the earth, we can't blame God. We need to look at who is not doing their part correctly. At the end of the day, we get the benefit of praying for God's will to be done on earth, and God is glorified as He intended it to be from day one.

Chapter 4

Speaking in tongues

The Bible talks about speaking in tongues, but what is *speaking in tongues*? How does one know they are speaking in tongues when they make the sounds that they do? This is a popular question asked by Christians and unbelievers alike. One reason is that people hide behind the saying, *God is working through me* or *God told me*. The reality is we don't have any real way of knowing if they are telling the truth, so we just let them be.

Some people say it's simply talking to God using a precise heavenly language that only God understands. There has been an ongoing debate about when this unknown language is given to individuals, either upon accepting Jesus as their Lord and Savior or being baptized with the Holy Spirit.

You have to ask for the gift of speaking in tongues because it does not just come upon you because you confess Jesus as Lord and his death, burial, and resurrection. That's what I have been told, anyway.

If you have been to a Pentecostal church like I have, you are bound to hear someone speaking in tongues. If you are like me, it sounds amazing, thought-provoking, and curious. This heavenly language is something I have been hearing since I was a child and have been drawn to ever since.

Some Christians may never speak in tongues, but that does not mean you never will. Also, it does not make you less of a Christian, but the ability to speak in tongues is something every Christian should seek. This is something that takes time and is a gift from God, not a requirement.

Since it's a gift, it has to be given, so you should be asking for the gift of speaking in tongues. It is also an indication that you are filled with the Holy Spirit, but not speaking in tongues does not mean you are not filled with the Holy Spirit.

Remember, the gift of speaking in tongues should be something you desire and are seeking from God. Also, receiving the gift might not happen immediately. A perfect walk in the Lord is not required to speak in tongues. There is no perfect person on the face of the earth. If there were, they would not need the Holy Spirit. If you want to speak in tongues, you must have the desire to accept the Holy Spirit and help from God.

The fact that I've never heard any two tongues sound alike when people speak in tongues leads me to believe that everyone has their own distinct language. I must say, a lot of Christians speaking in tongues do sound close to the point where they appear to be mimicking each other. How do I know that these tongue-speaking Christians are actually speaking a language and not just speaking gibberish?

The Bible says tongues are words that cannot be uttered. I don't need to know what is being said, but I do know that people can make sounds and say they are speaking in tongues when they are not.

The Bible talks about false prophets, so there are people who fake speaking in tongues. I have also asked tongue-speaking Christians to describe how they know that they are speaking in tongues, and no one gave a clear answer. The best they could tell me is that you will know it when you get the Holy Spirit. What kind of answer is that?

Paul says in 1 Corinthians 14:4 (NKJV):

He who speaks in tongues edifies himself, but he who prophesies edifies the church.

Paul is saying that speaking in tongues is not for asking God for something, but to uplift oneself in the Lord's will, which builds on your relationship with the Lord.

You can also say the main reason for speaking in tongues is to develop one's prayer life. I would be cautious of people who want to pray for you in tongues about your situation. If it were just to petition God for things, that would not make much sense since we can do so in our own earthly language. Notice that none of the significant biblical personalities ever petitioned God in tongues for anything personal.

Paul explains more (1 Corinthians 14:1-2, NKJV):

Pursue love, and desire spiritual gifts, but especially that you may prophesy. For he who speaks in a tongue does not speak to men but to God, for no one understands him; however, in the spirit he speaks mysteries.

What does *prophesy*[1] mean? It is a word of action to predict a divine inspiration or to preach. In today's English tongue, Paul is saying to chase after love and have a heart for the gifts of the Spirit, especially to preach the word of God. Sharing and proclaiming the word of God should be a priority in your life.

How were tongues used in the Bible? During the days of Paul, they spoke several languages, just like they do today. Paul himself spoke three languages. Acts 2:4 (NKJV) says:

And they were all filled with the Holy Spirit and began to speak with other tongues, as the Spirit gave them utterance.

The miracle was not speaking in a heavenly language that no one knows except God, but the tongues of fire, them being filled with the Holy Spirit, and them all receiving a language other than their native tongue without going to college or being taught by a bilingual.

The tongue they received was earthly and not

---

1. Merriam-Webster. (n.d.). *Prophesy*. In *Merriam-Webster.com dictionary*. Retrieved May 8, 2024, from https://www.merriam-webster.com/dictionary/prophesy

understood by someone who was not native to that language. If I try to hold a conversation with someone who only speaks Greek, no communication would be achieved because we don't speak the same language, even though we are speaking earthly languages to each other. If the disciples were supposed to go out and preach the word of the Lord, they would need to be able to communicate effectively to the masses, hence part of the reason for the new languages.

I want you to look at a few other times where tongues were spoken and mentioned in the Bible. Acts 10:44-46 and Acts 19:6 are two different occasions where the Holy Spirit fell on them before the tongue-speaking started.

Going back to 1 Corinthians, Paul emphasized prophesying rather than speaking an unknown language. When the Bible talks about prophecy, it refers to a person proclaiming the Holy Spirit, Jesus Christ, and the will of God.

Verse two states that when someone speaks in a tongue that is not understood by the listener, it is as if they are speaking directly to God, rather than the listener. This also means that to the man who understands a different language, the prophecy will be a mystery to his spirit since prophesying is for the spirit man.

Verse three is pretty much self-explanatory, and verse four confirms verse two. If a person speaks in a tongue not understood by the listener, they only edify themselves because they are the only ones understanding what they are saying.

The Bible says faith comes by hearing and hearing the word of God. It is not just by hearing the word of God, but by understanding what they hear. If someone interprets the tongues, they will edify the church because now the church can understand what's being said.

1 Corinthians 13:1 (NKJV) says:

Though I speak with the tongues of men and of angels, but have not love, I have become a sounding brass or a clanging cymbal.

To put this into perspective, Paul is saying I can speak eloquently and persuasively, delivering the Word of God and of angels, but if my actions and words are without love, all of my speaking is like banging on a cymbal, meaning nothing.

In verse five, Paul wishes everyone spoke a different language so they could reach more people, but Paul prefers that they prophesy and love. I believe the reason Paul prefers them to prophesy is that the person prophesying is bringing people to the knowledge of God, plus speaking in tongues is evidence for the unbeliever of being filled with the Holy Spirit. Remember, just because you don't see the evidence does not mean you aren't filled with the Holy Spirit. (Just because you have not seen my heart does not mean I don't have one.)

If you continue to read on from verse six to verse nineteen, you see Paul specifying the order in which tongues are supposed to be used in the church. He did that to avoid confusion (remember, God is not the author of confusion.)

Let's tackle this from a different angle. Have you ever found yourself praying and lost for words, or have a gut feeling that you are not praying what you should be praying? I have, and I would cry and groan out of frustration and desperation. To my surprise, the Bible actually speaks about groaning, something we do when we aren't sure what to pray for (as we ought to). The Holy Spirit translates our groaning to God. Romans 8:26-27 (NKJV) says:

Likewise, the Spirit also helps in our weaknesses. For we do not know what we should pray for as we ought, but the Spirit Himself makes intercession for us with groaning which cannot be uttered.

Crying is a form of communication to both man and God. It is the first form of communication known to man, and God knows exactly what is said through our crying.

Read Romans 8:26-27. Let me bring to your attention something people tend to miss when they read these verses. (I missed it the first few times I read it.) Think of the phrase *what we should pray for as we ought*. The verse is not saying we don't know what to pray for, but we don't know how to pray. Spiritually, we don't always know what we need to fulfill God's purpose for us. In a closer study, I discovered that it is not the Holy Spirit that is doing the groaning, but it is us. The Holy Spirit makes intercession for our groaning.

That groaning, I believe, is a form of speaking in tongues. Groanings cannot be uttered, and we don't know what is said. Based on the above verse, whatever form the tongue takes when it comes out of your mouth is not from your thoughts, nor can it be vocalized in a way we can understand.

The Holy Spirit is the one speaking in tongues using your mouth to utter the heavenly language you hear. Does that mean that every time a person groans, they are speaking in tongues? No. There are several reasons why people groan, often because of pain or frustration.

Here's something to consider: The sound that is coming out of your mouth should be words from a language that does not come from your own thoughts or native tongue. You still can hear what is coming out of your mouth and can repeat it later, groaning or not. The first time you spoke in tongues, you did not learn a complete language, but the Holy Spirit spoke through you with words of a heavenly language.

Let's talk about words and repetition. Whatever you are praying for when the Holy Spirit first speaks through you, it is unnecessary to repeat the words or sounds every time the Holy Spirit prays through you. Repeating the few words you heard doesn't mean you know the complete language spoken by the Holy Spirit. Plus, you may not be helping your situation because those words from the Holy Spirit may not line up with what you are praying about or for. Remember, the Holy Spirit speaks through us when He needs to, not the other way around, or you would be the one making the Holy Spirit speak at will.

From all the scriptures I've read about speaking in tongues, I have yet to come across any that describe the utterance I've heard in church and other places or what the tongue should sound like. My thoughts are this: after going over all the scriptures that I could find, tongues are words that cannot be uttered (emphasis on *cannot*).

If believers are uttering sounds that are formulated in a word-like sound, this does not add up to scripture. If a heavenly language is coming out of your mouth that cannot be uttered, it would have to be in the sound of groaning or another form that cannot be verbalized. With that being said, I'm not knocking anyone who makes the sound they make when they say that they are speaking in tongues. That is between them and the Lord.

If I repeat the sounds that a person makes when they speak in tongues, does that mean I spoke in tongues? If I repeat words from a person who speaks Spanish, French, or Japanese (which I don't), does that mean I just spoke a complete language? If I try to have a conversation with someone who speaks a foreign language, repeating the same few words I learned would not make any sense.

The same is true for people who make those repeated sounds and say they are speaking a heavenly language. The Holy Spirit is like a ventriloquist—the ventriloquist is the one who knows a language and talks using the mouth of the puppet. We are the puppet.

Chapter 5

The Trinity

When we talk about the trinity, the conversation can lead to a full-blown argument with some passionate verbal exchange, depending on who the conversation is with. It can sometimes lead to more confusion and disbelief. These types of conversations will never stop because we all have our own experiences and level of love for our creator and who we believe He is. Before we can come close to an agreement, we have to break down what is meant when we say *trinity* as it relates to God.

The word trinity does not appear in the Bible anywhere, but the concept of God the Father, Jesus the Son, and the Holy Spirit as one divine being is seen throughout the Bible. I will attempt to provide clarity on the subject and not inclusively define how God can be one being and all three at the same time. Isaiah 46:5 tells us that no one person can absolutely define the Father.

When most people use the word *god*, they use it as the name of our heavenly Father, like our government name. The word god is used to represent a position. There are several gods out there—Zeus, Aphrodite, Apollo, and Athena, just to name a few. Whether you think they are the true God, others do.

There are everyday objects or lifestyle things that people worship as gods. It is important to know this because the word god is used in the Bible sometimes carries a different meaning, even though it is spelled the same way.

The Bible refers to God as *anthropomorphic*. This means it starts with us at the bottom and works upward to say something significant about God, our Father. When we say God the Father, we are using His title in the representation of who He is, like when I say the *President of the United States of America*. Even if you don't know the actual name of that person, you still would know who I'm talking about.

Another thing to note is that the Bible was not written in English. The writers did not even set out to write what we know today as the Bible. The Bible is a compilation of letters to address different groups of people and individuals and to document events. Most importantly, the Bible is a book that outlines God's existence and His redemption plans for mankind.

Since English is a very modern language compared to the original Bible text, certain words do not directly translate into English. As a result, certain thoughts were not conveyed as originally intended. Punctuation was added based on the understanding of the original language and English grammar rules.

Remember, flawed men were responsible for putting the Bible together, and the translation may not have been inspired. Punctuations are not inspired, so misplaced punctuation can change the context of what was said. This is why you hear good pastors refer to the root word of a particular word to give it their best justice in explaining the scripture they are reading from.

Before I go any further, I want to ask this: When we say *one God*, what do we mean? If I say *one family*, does that mean only one individual exists in that family? No. A house has several rooms, all used for different purposes, but it is still one house. So, to fully understand the trinity of God, logic, and critical thinking will only get you so far. You have to ask God the Father to reveal what He meant by He is one God, but there is also Jesus and the Holy Spirit.

When people try to explain the trinity, they fail to realize that each person of the trinity functions in a specific role and does not contradict the other. Because of their role, people think they are separate individuals, while some think that they function as fully God the Father in each role.

When the universe was being created, God the Father was in His full Father role. Once He started in the role of Jesus, God the Father only assisted. When He finished the role of Jesus, He started the role of the Holy Spirit, even though sometimes all three are working in their respective role at the same time.

Think about it: God the Father has finished creating, so His major role is not in action. Jesus' role has shifted to intercession while He sits on the right hand of God. The Holy Spirit is the one who is playing a major role right now, bringing back things to our remembrance, comforting, and empowering us.

Genesis 1:1 (NKJV) says:

In the beginning, God created the heavens and the earth.

John 1:1-2 (NKJV) says:

In the beginning was the Word, and the Word was with God, and the Word was God. He was in the beginning with God.

In Genesis, the Bible uses the title *God,* while in John 1, the Bible lets you know that this title was given to the creator of the heavens and the earth. It also uses *with God* and *was God*, showing there is more than one person here at work. This does not take away from the oneness of God (remember the family example I used).

Notice that the person having the title God is spoken of as saying, *In the beginning God created…* Then in John 1:1-2, the same God is talked about as *And the Word was with God and the Word was God.* This tells me that there is more than one person at work here, but at the same time, proving His oneness. If God could not do that, then that would mean He can't do all things, which is not true. Remember, God the

Father is not human, so human terminology can hardly do any justice in explaining His fullness.

In Genesis 1:26a (NKJV):

Then God said, "Let Us make man in Our image, according to Our likeness."

This tells me that the Father, Jesus, and the Holy Spirit, who are included in *Our,* have a form similar to my physical and spiritual form. This is the first true physical form of a description we have of the Father, the head person in the Trinity. If we could look at Him with the naked eye, we would see He can have a form like me and not some alien with wings wearing a toga outfit.

If you notice in Genesis 1:27b (NKJV), He said:

In the image of God He created him; male and female He created them.

Wow! A female is *him* as well, so is God both male and female? No, He is not a female but is a spirit, as the Bible says. Being the only true and living God, He can do that. Remember, we established that one does not always negate singular as in 1, 2, 3.

When the Bible says God made us in the image of God, it is mainly talking about our spiritual form. Even though He is not always in a human form, He is sometimes in the form of fire or whatever the shape of wind is.

I want you to note that the Father does not have a name like Jesus, the physical or flesh form of the Trinity, as most people would refer to him. Exodus 3:14 (NKJV) says:

And God said to Moses, "I AM WHO I AM." And He said, "Thus you shall say to the children of Israel, 'I AM has sent me to you."

What does this mean? Is this really a name? It depends on the angle at which you approach this topic. If you are looking at it as if it is supposed to be an earthly name, then I would say you are wrong. God is not an earthly being, and our earthly language is limited in describing anything outside of time. God gave us the only words on earth that best capture who He is.

Also, God is not bound by anything, and to give Him an earthly name would be limiting who He is. There is no timeline implied in the words *I AM*, as they exist in a continuous present without a defined start or finish.

Numbers 23:19 (NKJV) tells us that:

God is not a man, that He should lie, Nor a son of man, that He should repent. Has He said, and will He not do? Or has He spoken, and will He not make it good?

We share some of God's characteristics as humans, but He does not operate in the capacity of those characteristics as we do. Remember, in the book of Genesis, we are created in His image and not the other way around, which means all of our ways, attitudes, emotions, and feelings should mirror His. He has them, too, just at a righteous level.

Some of the humanistic ways of God are that He thinks, talks, grieves, etc. He loves, and He is love. He can get angry, and He is also a jealous God.

The book of Exodus talks about this and confirms that there are many gods. In 20:3 (NKJV):

You shall have no other gods before Me.

This statement declares that there are gods other than God the Father and shows His jealousy. So you can see He is not much different from you and me, except that He is flawless and righteous.

Unlike you and me, God has no race or ethnicity. First of all, there is only one race, the human race, but many shades of complexion. People seem to think that there is more than one race because of the color of a person's skin. Your skin color does not determine your race.

Think about this: the Bible says God is a Spirit. John 4:24 (NKJV) tells us that:

> *God is Spirit, and those who worship Him must worship in spirit and truth.*

Who is a spirit? The best way I can articulate this with limited human capabilities is that the Holy Spirit is a helper; He is truth, invisible, invincible, and He is power. Those are just some of the ways we can describe the Holy Spirit.

Act 1:8 talks about power, specifically the power of God. Jesus is speaking to His disciples and others, saying that they will receive power when the Holy Spirit comes upon them; therefore, the Holy Spirit is power.

The disciples only received power after the Holy Spirit came upon them, which is safe to say the Holy Spirit was indeed present and active in their lives. The first conclusion is that a spirit is invisible. They did not have the power that they were going to receive before the Holy Spirit came upon them.

Based on Acts 1:8, the Holy Spirit is an invisible power that can be placed on someone or even carry out a task without the help of anyone. A similar event happened to the Virgin Mary. In Luke's account of the virgin conception of Jesus, the same thing happened: the Holy Spirit came upon her and the power of the Highest will overshadow her.

So you can see a spirit can do human things and things that humans cannot do. They use us to do things not because they cannot do it by themselves, but because we are the ones who need the help. They also have the ability and the power to do those things which they intend to do. Hopefully, I have clarified some concerns you had.

Now that we have a better understanding of who God the Father is and what He is not, let's look at who Jesus is. Before I go any further, let me remind you of the house analogy: there is one house, but different parts of the house, and that does not change the fact that it's one house.

The Bible talks about one God who is described in a triune way, frequently causing people to confuse function with a person. This confusion makes it much more difficult to explain one God with a triune distinction. Jesus is called the Son of God several times in the Bible. This is not comparable to the human birthing process. Jesus is not lower or lesser compared to God the Father; rather, Jesus is one part of the same house, providing a specific function.

Although Jesus admits that He is the Son of God, the term "Son" also refers to a title of position in the Trinity. This is the way God the Father distinguishes between the function of the Father, Jesus, and the Holy Spirit. In Matthew 6:9-13, the first line says, *Our Father in heaven.* Jesus saying *our Father* is an inclusion of himself. From that statement, you can distinguish Jesus, his function, the Father, and the fact that Jesus is the Son, as he said himself.

Why is Jesus referred to as a child and a son? This is because, as a human, he was born as a child with flesh and blood with a human body. When he is referred to as a son, it tells us he was already in existence for him to be given. Isaiah 9:6 (NKJV) confirms this for us:

For unto us a Child is born, Unto us a Son is given;

And the government will be upon His shoulder. And His name will be called Wonderful, Counselor, Mighty God, Everlasting Father, Prince of Peace.

These two terms are used to describe the same person but with several responsibilities.

The word child here highlights God in human form, having the authority to do His will on earth legally. The letter "C" in child is capitalized to represent Jesus' birth, and the capitalization of "S" emphasizes his preexistence and ability to be given.

Jesus is what you call *hypostases*—the single person of Christ, as contrasted with his dual nature as human and divine. This is reflected by the way the Bible presents his names: when *Jesus* appears in front of the word *Christ*, it is referring to his human side, and when *Christ* appears in front of *Jesus*, it is referring to his divine nature.

The thing that is hard to believe is that God cannot do anything on the earth legally without the use of a human being. This is not because He can't do so, but because He will not violate His word He set in the earth from the time of creation. If He violates His word, He will lose His credibility and trust. When the Bible uses the word Son, it is referring to the deity side of Jesus. With that said, we can now talk about the deity side of Jesus or the human side.

Focusing on the human side of Him, why did God need a human body? To answer that question, I have to go back to the beginning of creation. Before God created the world, He, the angels, and the other extraterrestrial beings existed in heaven. So when the Bible says *in the beginning*, it is talking about when God started creating the physical world.

Think about this: When an architect decides to design a building, the creation of that building starts from a thought and then moves to the drafting table. So did the world.

I say that to let you know that things were happening in the heavenly realm long before the creation of Earth. How do I know this? Isaiah 14:12 (NKJV) says:

How you are fallen from heaven, O Lucifer, son of the morning! How you are cut down to the ground, You who weakened the nations!

Based on what Isaiah said, a lot of things were going on in heaven, including the thought of creating the earth. What nations did Lucifer weaken, and what ground did he get cut down to? Keep in mind God is omniscient, knowing all things, so when He created the earth and mankind, He knew they would fall because of the devil.

Genesis 2:17 (NKJV) says:

But of the tree of the knowledge of good and evil you shall not eat, for in the day that you eat of it you shall surely die. Notice what God did not say. He did not say, *If you eat of the tree of knowledge of good and evil, you shall surely die.*

That would be an indication that God didn't know Adam was going to eat from the tree, which would mean that God is not omniscient. With all this going on, the devil is upset about being kicked out of heaven and wants to get back at God through His creation.

Because God knew they would eat from the tree, He devised a plan to reconcile us back to Him when they did. Eating from the tree separated us from God. To redeem us back to God, the plan would have to allow God to operate legally on the earth without violating His words that He used to create the earth and the systems of the earth. With His word in place and the earth being given to the devil by the man Adam, the devil now has the authority to run the system. God cannot do whatever He wants whenever He wants.

Take note of this also: the devil does not have a flesh and blood body like Jesus did, and he cannot create one. That is why he is in this world as a spiritual influencer and using demands to possess the human bodies who are unaware of his tricks and those who will let him.

God loves us so much that He was not going to let us stay under the authority of the devil. That's where His plan comes into effect. John 3:16 (NKJV) says it all:

For God so loved the world that He gave His only begotten Son, that whoever believes in Him should not perish but have everlasting life.

Let us look at what God is saying here. He is saying that the love He has for us is not just surface love. God's love is a deep, emotional agape love (that is why it is worded *so loved*). It shows the level and degree of love He has for us.

I also want to point out that when the verse says *the world*, it does not include the perverted systems that Satan caused. It is talking about the world before the devil perverted it.

What God did next was to prove His love by giving His only begotten son, Jesus, to redeem us from the clutches of the devil. That act was putting Himself into the perverted system Satan caused, allowing Himself to die by the system of this world. God had to do that to regain the authority of the world and mankind. Executing all this is just a peek into God's extreme divinity.

The process of doing that requires a blood sacrifice, which we as humans cannot fulfill because of the nature of the transaction. This transaction involves extraterrestrial matters and requires a supernatural transaction that none of us can do. Human involvement is necessary to restore power on earth, which is where Jesus comes into play.

Jesus was born into this world, which made him a human and still God. God gave us a part of Himself (*the Word*), Jesus, in a flesh form, which is mentioned in the beginning of the book of John.

So you can see Jesus is a human deity, and while he was walking on earth, he operated as such. If Jesus were to operate in any other capacity, it would be a lie and ask us to do things we cannot do.

Before the beginning, the devil became the envy of God. Isaiah 14:12-15 tells us this is a sin, and God cannot allow sin to run rampant in His kingdom. Satan's envy ultimately drove him to target one of God's greatest possessions, us, which he is using to get back at God for his expulsion from heaven.

The devil knows something about Jesus being born on earth as a human, which is a restriction God imposed on Himself. With this restriction, it gives God the right to operate as a human in the world and not break His law. The devil believed killing Jesus would be his way to seek revenge against God. That is why, from the day Jesus was born, the devil was seeking to kill him. What the devil didn't know was that God intended for Jesus to die as a human to accomplish our redemption.

Since Jesus was now operating as a human, he needed the help of mankind to complete the job he came here for. Remember, after His virgin birth, when he was about two years old, his earthly parents had to flee from where they were living. The devil influenced Herod, the ruling king, to kill all boys around Jesus' age group when he learned of His birth. This act of fleeing shows how vulnerable Jesus was as a human and how the devil CANNOT kill whoever he wants or whenever he wants.

With that said, don't think for one second that God could not protect His Son, Jesus. God can do so, but because He will not violate His word, He uses the help of man. How else would He prove that Jesus was still a man?

The book of Genesis reveals that the devil, an extraterrestrial, cannot freely operate on earth without a body, despite being granted authority by man. Unlike God our Father, he cannot perform miracles like God our Father did. The devil can only influence us through our thoughts, ideas, and suggestions.

As you read the Bible, you will notice that Jesus did pretty much everything like us humans without sinning—eat, sleep, work, abide by the earthly laws, and give thanks. There are plenty of other times the Bible shows us that he was a human. In Luke chapter 2, there is a story about Jesus as a young boy attending a Passover feast in Jerusalem. His parents grew concerned when they realized he wasn't with the family. It turns out that he was talking with the teachers in the temple.

Verse 52 (NKJV) says:

And Jesus increased in wisdom and stature, and in favor with God and men.

If he were operating in his divinity and was omniscient, in what way could he increase in wisdom and stature? This just shows you he was all human and all God at the same time.

As a deity, he is more than we can imagine, and then some. Whatever the Bible says about God is already clear. While He operated as a human on earth, God the Father did some things through Jesus that could only be done through him because he was sinless. Remember, if Jesus did anything on earth through his divine nature, he would violate God's word, and that would defeat the reason for coming to earth.

Let's look at the miracle of Jesus walking on water. This miracle requires the suspension of the law of gravity. If you get a person who you think is the most faithful man on earth, including yourself, you cannot duplicate that miracle without an anointing for that specific miracle.

If someone doesn't possess the anointing, they will be walking on the bottom of the pool, the ocean, or wherever they attempt this miracle. A big part of us not being able to do that today is the fact that God does not need that type of miracle in this time and age.

The next miracle I want to examine is when Jesus rose from the dead. What is so different about this compared to when other people in the Bible were resurrected from the dead? Everybody else who rose from the dead needed someone to raise them from the dead, but Jesus needed no one. He raised himself from the dead, being that he is God in the flesh. Unlike the others who were raised from the dead and died again, Jesus will not. No one can do that kind of miracle, regardless of how much faith they have.

With a clear understanding of two members of the tribune, let's focus on the next. Who is the Holy Spirit? Before I even attempt to answer this question, let me first say that He is just another person of the tribune nature of God the Father. I purposely did not say the third person of God because putting a place of position on the Holy Spirit implies that there is a level of strength, priority, or importance between the triune God. There is no first, second, or third person of God because He is one.

Also, keep in mind that what you are about to read is not all-inclusive of who he is. We do not have the vocabulary to describe the Holy Spirit accurately. The Holy Spirit is the one person of the Godhead that no one has seen in a human form with the naked eye anywhere throughout the Bible. Moses caught a glimpse of God's backside in a human form, and people saw and touched Jesus during His time on earth as a human. The same cannot be said about the Holy Spirit.

Luke 3:22 (NKJV) states:

And the Holy Spirit descended in bodily form like a dove upon Him, and a voice came from heaven which said, "You are My beloved Son; in You I am well pleased."

As you can see, even though the Holy Spirit can take on a physical form, he is not always portrayed in that state of being. The Holy Spirit has also appeared in the form of fire. Acts 2:3 (NKJV) says:

Then there appeared to them divided tongues, as of fire, and one sat upon each of them.

The Holy Spirit is distinguished from God the Father and Jesus the Son in a unique way. He can be poured out, fill you, live within you, reveal things, guide you, overtake you, and possess power, among other things. There is no end to the ways in which you can recognize the Holy Spirit.

In my conversations and debates with theologian college professors, church brothers, coworkers, friends, and family members, I sometimes use water as an analogy to explain how the Holy Spirit has revealed himself to me. Water can be in three forms: solid, liquid, and gas. God the Father would be the liquid, the main source, which can become ice. Jesus the Son is the ice, and the Holy Spirit would be the gas. The one God, our Father, expresses Himself in three ways.

This is why Jesus can talk and refer to God and the Holy Spirit as if they are three different people. Think about this for a minute: when we mention the word *water*, steam or ice doesn't necessarily come to mind, even though you can get both from water.

The things that water can do, steam or gas cannot, and vice versa, because of the state it is in. Steam will not flood your neighborhood street, nor will you drink steam. That doesn't change the fact that it is still water in a different form. If you look at it from that perspective, you will get a better understanding of the Holy Trinity and a better perspective of the Holy Spirit.

John 1:1 (NKJV):

The Trinity

In the beginning was the Word, and the Word was with God, and the Word was God.

Genesis 1:26a (NKJV):

Then God said, "Let Us make man in Our image, according to Our likeness.

The *us* that the scripture is referring to is God the Father, God the Jesus, and God the Holy Spirit, who are one. So whenever you talk about God, it is very important to make sure you are specific about which part of the trinity you are talking about because they all do different things and are in different states of being.

No part of the tribune is more God than the other because they are the same person. In the grand scheme of things, when it comes to the beginning and the end, God's work is done.

After God created the world and all that's in it, He rested (granted, most of that work was just by talking). God did some more work here and there throughout the Old Testament. Then Jesus' part of the redemption work started with the birth until his death, burial, and resurrection, and then his part of the job was done. Jesus is not doing anything else right now but sitting down at the right hand of God, waiting on us to make the devil his footstool as he makes intercessions for us.

Psalm 110:1 tells us this:

The Lord said to my Lord, "Sit at My right hand, Till I make Your enemies Your footstool."

So from the time he went back to heaven, he's been sitting down. The Holy Spirit is now responsible for all the work on God's side of things. We are doing our part of the work with the help of the Holy Spirit.

Hopefully, I have given you a little more clarity on the tribune God. Everyone should pray and ask God for revelation and explanation to have a better understanding of him.

Chapter 6

The Power of Words

The next thing I want to talk to you about may seem trivial or pointless to some people: *words*. Words are one of the most powerful things in the universe, if not the most powerful thing given to man.

Here on Earth, you can cause things to happen halfway around the world using words. From Earth, you can cause things to happen in heaven. Humans, from the beginning of existence, used words to communicate, destroy, and create.

Words transcend the time dimension. The Bible even tells you that words will be forever. According to Proverbs 18:21 (NKJV), *death and life are in the power of the tongue.* Life or death is in the words we speak, so we need to know how to use our words.

When the Bible was removed from schools and government buildings, it was just as if we had taken the pencils and pens out of the hands of children and replaced them with a nuclear bomb detonator. But did they really take the Word of God out of those places? No. As long as you have teachers and students believing in the Word of God, He is still there.

Words are more than just the sounds we make when we speak or sing; they are a reflection of our thoughts. In their simplest form, words serve as a means of communication, allowing us to express ourselves in various ways. They have the power to create and destroy.

Have you ever stopped to consider the true nature of *words*? I have, and I realize that words cannot be accurately described as merely the sounds we make when we talk. We often quote the Bible, but no words are heard when we read the Bible in silence. So, what are words exactly, and why are we talking about them? The Bible discusses words in various ways, emphasizing their significance.

Ephesians 4:29 (NKJV) says:

Let no corrupt word proceed out of your mouth, but what is good for necessary edification, that it may impart grace to the hearers.

Paul is letting us know we cannot just say the first thing that comes to mind. Note that he is telling us not to let corrupt words come out of our mouths, versus telling us *to ask God* to not let corrupt words come out of our mouths.

Let's dig deeper into what the Bible says about words. When most Christians hear the *Word*, their thoughts automatically go to the Bible, as the Bible is known as the *Word of God*. But even the phrase is open to interpretation.

Does the *Word of God* mean that God spoke all the words written in the Bible, that the Bible is all about God, or that the Bible is inspired by God? When a person says the Bible is the Word of God, they clarify what they are saying. You cannot have a meaningful conversation without first qualifying the basis of the discussion. Also, keep in mind that the Bible has words in it that are spoken by the devil and many people.

Did you know that in the entire first chapter of Genesis, the Lord only spoke nine times? Look at the number of words that are in chapter 1. In the Bible, the *Word* is spoken of as a person, as life. It can go forth, do things, communicate, and create, just to mention a few.

God's Word is how we strengthen our relationship with Father God. To get a better understanding, we have to consult the Bible, the place where all this started. We will start at the beginning of Genesis, chapter 1.

Initially, God created the universe by speaking. Genesis 1:3b (NKJV):

Let there be Light.

Some argue it was because God could not see or wanted to create light (remember, God is light). Either way, words were spoken and, as because of those spoken words, light came into existence. (Side Note: When God said *let there be light*, He was not creating the sun.)

As you can see, words can cause an effect once spoken. God thought not only of light but verbalized it, which is how light came into existence. This shows that words have an effect once spoken, rather than just thought about. While words can affect the person thinking them, they do not affect anyone else until spoken aloud. If you continue reading Genesis chapter 1, you will see that God created other things by speaking them into existence.

God's word differs greatly from ours, despite their similar powers. We can't make physical things happen when we speak, so we will not create anything like God did with His words. One of the best things we can do with words is to say what God says about our situation because His words will not come back to Him void. Isaiah 55:11 (NKJV) says:

So shall My word be that goes forth from My mouth; it shall not come back to Me void, But it shall accomplish what I please, And it shall prosper in the thing for which I sent it.

The Bible talks about God's word in two main ways —Logos and Rhema. Logos and Rhema are Greek words that mean utterance in English. So, what is the significant difference in the Bible using two different words to say the same thing? Let's look at Logos first. John 1:1 (NKJV) says:

In the beginning was the Word and the Word was with God, and the Word was God.

In this sentence, those three words refer to Jesus before he took on flesh.

Other places in the Bible where this can be seen are John 4:37 and John 5:38. As it pertains to Rhema, John 3:34, John 6:63, and John 6:68 reference that. So hopefully you can see the differences between God's words (and how they relate to Him) and the spoken word.

One big part of a Christian's life is praying, and to pray, you have to use words (whether verbally or sign language). The Bible tells us several times that when communicating with God effectively, speaking is always required, regardless of the form used.

One of the many actions of communicating with God is called praying. The Bible tells us that when we pray, we should ask and it shall be given, and we ought to praise the Lord. You cannot do any of those things without the utterance of words, sign language, or gestures.

God's word expressed in another form is found in John 1:14a (KJV):

And the Word was made flesh, and dwelt among us.

That verse lets me know that the Word has taken on another form other than sound, which is flesh. Now this type of word differs from all other words because it has a human entity and was in existence from the time of God. Why do I say this? Because John continues to say the Word was God and the Word was with God.

When you study the Bible, you will learn that when God speaks, it is always with purpose and for a purpose. Matthew 8:16 (NKJV) tells us:

and He cast out the spirits with a word, and healed all who were sick.

From that scripture, you see that Jesus didn't *think* of healing or *think* the evil spirits out, but *cast* them out. He *spoke* what he wanted and he used his words. Note in that scripture that sickness can hear, and the spirit does as well. If the word was not uttered, sickness and the evil spirit would not have heard it and been compelled by the authority of the words that were spoken.

God does not speak idle words like we do. Can you imagine God doing that? In the same way God speaks with a purpose, we should do the same because our words have life, authority, and power, and should be used with wisdom.

The Bible says we will have to give an account for every idle word we utter, not some of it, but every word. Matthew 12:36, 37 (NKJV) tells us:

But I say to you that for every idle word men may speak, they will give account of it in the day of judgment. For by your words you will be justified, and by your words you will be condemned.

After knowing this, what are idle words? Idle words are empty rhetoric. Ask yourself: *What empty rhetoric have I spit out since I've been talking?*

If we have to give an account for every idle word we speak, it would behoove us to be mindful of the things we say. Words hold such significance to God that we will be judged based on them. So if we care about our lives, we won't speak idle words in ignorance.

Do you remember everything you said since your first word? How much of it is idle?

It is not just idle words that we have to be careful about, but also words that open doors to evil in your life or the lives of others. Ephesians 4:29 (NIV) says:

Do not let any unwholesome talk come out of your mouths, but only what is helpful for building others up according to their needs, that it may benefit those who listen.

Be mindful of what you tell people or yourself. Words have life, and you should speak life and not death over your life and others.

Words are so closely related to speaking in tongues that to utter words, you need the use of your tongue. For people who are not mute and are at the talking age, we are constantly talking, some more than others. Talking can be very detrimental to the hearer and speaker.

James 3:3 tells us how untamable the tongue is, so think before you speak. When you talk, are you saying good or bad things? You can read the Bible and find where people say things that are not considered good, depending on your viewpoint.

Proverbs 18:21 (NKJV) says:

> *Death and life are in the power of the tongue, And those who love it will eat its fruit.*

This is a perfect example of the importance of words, their strength, and how much more it is than just sounds coming out of your mouth.

The words that come out of your mouth can either give life or cause death. When words are spoken, they carry a lot of power and will affect the hearer, including the speaker, and even someone who didn't hear them. According to Genesis 9:25 (NKJV):

Then he said: "Cursed be Canaan; A servant of servants He shall be to his brethren."

Here you can see a human being exercising the power of words across generations. Notice that Noah spoke a curse on Ham's child, Canaan, but Ham and Noah were the ones who heard what was said. Canaan had not been born, but the words spoken affected his life.

This reminds me of a saying I used to hear a lot when I was growing up. *Sticks and stones might break my bones, but words cannot hurt me.* If that was not the dumbest thing I heard. At the time, I did not know what I was really saying until I grew up and gave it some thought. The truth is words will hurt you just as much as a stick or stone, and sometimes even more.

In the same way that the power of words can work negatively on a person who does not hear the words spoken over them, it positively works the same. That's why you should speak positive, encouraging, and uplifting words to your kids, whether they hear them or not.

I would like to look at another event in the Bible that highlights the power of the Word and the close relationship words have with faith. Matthew 17:20 (NKJV):

So Jesus said to them, "Because of your unbelief; for assuredly, I say to you, if you have faith as a mustard seed, you will say to this mountain, 'Move from here to there,' and it will move; and nothing will be impossible for you."

Notice how Jesus ended with *and nothing will be impossible for you*. He was using what would be impossible in the physical world, compared to what can seem likely in circumstances in life, and persecution from the world. Words have the power to change that.

God is showing you that words, when used correctly, can do what seems impossible. Also, note the need to have faith and faith in what you are saying. Faith is ineffective unless you vocalize what you have faith in.

According to Jesus, the size of your faith does not matter; your words and corresponding actions do. The measure of faith lies not in its size or level but in how challenging it is to accept God's truth over our instincts.

Hebrews 4:12 (NKJV) tells us:

For the word of God is living and powerful, and sharper than any two-edged sword, piercing even to the division of soul and spirit, and of joints and marrow, and is a discerner of the thoughts and intents of the heart.

In this verse, the writer is describing what the word of God can do. First, it is living and powerful, and its effectiveness is compared to a two-edged sword. This means that God's words are likened to a weapon that can cause harm to the flesh, the soul, and the spirit. A sword can also be used to defend. How powerful!

The verse also said that the word is living, which means it accomplishes whatever it sets out to do 100% of the time. It also has wisdom, knowledge, and understanding of our thoughts and intent, which are of the mind and heart.

The sword's dual-edged description implies its effectiveness in spoken and heard situations, benefiting the user when used according to God's will. If God's word can do all that, wouldn't it be wise of us to use it in our everyday lives?

Living forever is a conversation or a thought that all of us will have at some point in our lives, if not already. Unbelievers and certain believers often associate the phrase *live forever* with the physical body, depending on the context. The spirit man is the part of man that will live forever, whether in heaven or in the lake of fire. Mostly when God talks about man, He is referring to the spirit man.

To live forever, you will have to refer to the real you, the spirit you. For the flesh to sustain life, you must feed it with the nutrients it requires—physical food. Like the flesh man, the spirit man also needs to be fed. What do you feed the spirit? The Bible tells us this in Matthew 4:4 (NKJV):

But He answered and said, "It is written, 'Man shall not live by bread alone, but by every word that proceeds from the mouth of God.'"

Meditating on those words, you can see that Jesus is speaking, and he is not talking about the hunger one gets from not eating bread, even though that's what the devil was talking about. Jesus directed his statement towards the spirit of man, as words cannot be consumed as physical food.

The Bible offers plenty of food for the spirit man. This is partly the reason why God doesn't just talk for the sake of it. John 6:35 (NKJV) also tells us what the Spirit eats:

And Jesus said to them, "I am the bread of life. He who comes to Me shall never hunger, and he who believes in Me shall never thirst."

Jesus is saying he is the Word of God, and if you believe in him, you will never lack the source of spiritual food.

We covered a lot in discussing words and haven't scratched the surface. We would not be doing this topic any justice if we did not talk about bad words, if there is such a thing.

You can almost be sure that if you ask ten people from different cultures to describe what bad words are, there will be quite a few inconsistencies in their answers. This is based on several factors, ranging from culture and social effects to spiritual beliefs, just to name a few. Studying American taboo words reveals their varying impact and meaning across cultures.

If you should pay attention to offensive language across cultures, you'll see that it either loses its impact or amplifies its intended effect. I believe the most used bad word is *f@#k*. Similar to other curse words, this word is just an ordinary word when used alone or in its proper context. Curse words and profanities are not the same, but people use them synonymously (please don't make that mistake).

Ephesians 5:4 (NKJV) tells us:

Neither filthiness, nor foolish talking, nor coarse jesting, which are not fitting, but rather giving of thanks.

Read Ephesians 5:1-7 to get a full grasp of the content.

I believe the word *f@#k* is popular because of the various ways it can be expressed—in surprise, pain, anger, contempt, pleasure, hate, etc.—and to express love. Is the word bad or the meaning that the use of the word projects? One of the unfortunate things about bad words is that people can make up their own as they see fit. One interesting thing I noticed about the bad words used in Western cultures and a few other parts of the world is that it has a sexual or animalistic connotation to them.

Then, some people have no regard for the actual words they choose to use in certain situations. Some people don't even care where they use them or who they direct them to. Some people would say, *god*

The Meaning of Life and Faith

d@*nit or *Jesus Christ*, not considering the words they just uttered. Those words themselves are not bad, but the combination and the intent with which they are used make them bad.

Pastors have to be careful how they use the words *hell* and *ass* on the pulpit, even though those words are found in the Bible and used by Jesus. That's how crazy it gets with speaking good or evil.

So why do people feel the need to use those words to express themselves? Sometimes they want to emphasize the seriousness of their intent. They want your trust in what they are saying, as if they have the final say on the matter. This is more recognized, especially when they swear by something—their mother's grave, the heavens, or God.

Matthew 5:33-37 (NKJV) says:

Again you have heard that it was said to those of old, 'You shall not swear falsely, but shall perform your oaths to the Lord.' But I say to you, do not swear at all: neither by heaven, for it is God's throne; nor by the earth, for it is His footstool; nor by Jerusalem, for it is the city of the great King. Nor shall you swear by your head, because you cannot make one hair white or black. But let your 'Yes' be 'Yes,' and your 'No,' 'No.' For whatever is more than these is from the evil one.

Jesus is telling us there is no need to swear or use bad words for any reason to express ourselves, and why we shouldn't do it. These verses are also letting people know they should not go prophesying, saying God told them anything He did not.

Take the word *stupid*. This word cannot be expressed in as many ways as the previous word, *f@#k*. I am not an English scholar, but I have never heard anyone use the word stupid in a good way. In my mind, that's a bad word. From now on, I encourage you to be mindful of what you say, the words you use, and how you use them.

Let's all be more conscious of how we speak about others and what we speak over others and ourselves. There is a lot more that can be said about words, but it is now up to you to seek that knowledge. You can start by reading the book of Proverbs.

Now that your mind is focused on words, I want to address some popular sayings believers use that are not biblical or nonsensical. These sayings can slowly disintegrate our faith or even take us out of faith and alignment with God.

One of the favorite sayings that I grew up hearing was *cleanliness is next to godliness*. As I started reading my Bible with much more understanding and attentiveness, I realized this phrase is nowhere in the Bible. I think people wanted to believe that if they were clean, that would bring them closer to God or, maybe, God wouldn't see how dirty their hearts were.

The next saying is *God helps those who help themselves*. If that's not one of the most idiotic things I have ever heard, I don't know what is. If you can help yourself, then what would you need God for? Psalms 121:2 (NKJV) says:

> *My help comes from the LORD, Who made heaven and earth.*

Now do you see how far from the truth that saying is? This kind of verbiage only weakens your faith, and as a Christian, if you don't have faith, you have nothing. If God only helps those who help themselves, what would happen to those who cannot help themselves? Who and where would they get help from?

Often, I would hear Christians say things that weaken their faith. Saying things like *God may not come when you want Him, but He is always on time*. When you say things like that, you are limiting God to human abilities when He is not a human.

If God is omnipresent, where would He be coming from? Even though the premise is that He will always make a way at the right time, by using that popular saying, you are giving life to the wrong words. What you are really doing is like playing a basketball game with baseball rules. That is an indication that you don't recognize who God is, which stems from a lack of faith in God.

God should be inside you as the Holy Spirit, confirming that God isn't *coming* from anywhere. Furthermore, if He is going to *show up on time,* wouldn't that mean that it does not matter when we want Him to show up since He will be there before the enemy has his way?

Another thing to consider is if God does not show up when you want Him, what would be the point of Him showing up? Plus, if He is going to show up on time, wouldn't that mean it does not matter when we want Him to show up since He will show up on His own timing?

God will provide is another popular saying that people don't realize how far from faith the saying is. A saying like this shines the light on a Christian's faith and how much they understand and apply the Word of God to their life, especially their prayer life.

The first two words of that saying are problematic for me. To say *God will* means God is going to do something that He has not yet done. According to Mark 11:24 (NKJV):

Therefore, I say to you, whatever things you ask when you pray, believe that you receive them, and you will have them.

There is nothing in Jesus' statement that indicates God does not already have what you are asking for and that He needs to go and get what you are praying for. The reason is that it's already in existence, whether in the spirit realm or right here in the earthly realm.

2 Peter 1:3 (NKJV) says:

As His divine power has given to us all things that pertain to life and godliness, through the knowledge of Him who called us by glory and virtue.

Note the past tense, indicating it is already done. The same thing goes for healing. The Bible says *by His Stripes we were healed*, meaning we already have it, we just need to align our faith with His words.

Don't forget that praying is not something we do to make God do something. It is we who need to receive what God has provided for us.

God will not give us more than we can bear. Is that even in the Bible? No, it's not! If God is the one causing our problems, then what role does the devil play? Plus, why would God burden us, and then tell us to bring our burdens to receive rest? He would be contradicting Himself (read Psalms 55:22 and James 1:13 for an explanation).

1 Corinthians 10:13 (NKJV) says:

> *No temptation has overtaken you except such as is common to man; but God is faithful, who will not allow you to be tempted beyond what you are able, but with the temptation will also make the way of escape, that you may be able to bear it.*

In the first part of that verse, the Bible tells us that the temptation we go through is common to man. The second part lets us know that God is faithful to NOT let us be tempted beyond what we can, plus He will show us a way of escape. I want you to zoom in on the word *tempted* and notice it did not say He would tempt us.

If you read the entire chapter 10 of 1 Corinthians, you will see that there are a lot of sinful things the Bible tells us not to do, meaning we have free will, and these are not things God is doing to us. So if you are going through issues caused by any of those sins, there is always a way out.

Saying that God will not give you more than you can bear is wrong. That is not a reason for you to think that the issues of life result from God tempting you or putting any burden on you. What would be the purpose of God tempting you?

God is not giving us problems; it is our not being obedient to the things He told us and the devil trying to *steal, kill, and destroy* us that gives us problems. The worst part of that is we expect God to bail us out. When He lets the consequences of our actions play out, we complain, asking why God let bad things happen to us. We need to stop saying that and be mindful of our words.

Often, I hear unbelievers and Christians say *no devil in hell* or *not even the devil in hell* could do *so and so*. Believing that the devil is in hell is exactly what the devil wants you to believe, along with the idea that God is in charge of everything going on in the world systems. If He is in charge, then He is responsible for the problems you are going through. To say *no devil in hell* is presuming that there are several devils in hell and one of them is causing the issues you are talking about. That could be true if you were in hell with them.

Whether you refer to him as the devil or Satan, I can assure you he is not in hell, not right now, anyway. The first time we learned of him was in the book of Genesis 3:3 when he tempted Eve to eat the fruit. He did not tempt her from hell; he was right there in the Garden of Eden, a place on earth that God set apart for Adam. Other scriptures in the Bible that prove he is not in hell, like Job 1:7 (NKJV):

And the Lord said to Satan, "From where do you come?" So Satan answered the Lord and said, "From going to and fro on the earth, and from walking back and forth on it."

Satan himself told us that he was not in hell. Notice he did not tell God that he came from hell. The surprising thing for me is that he still has access to come into the Lord's presence. You would think that once he got kicked out of heaven, he would have lost all access to be in the presence of God. 1 Peter 5:8 (NKJV) also confirms the devil is not in hell.

Be sober, be vigilant; because your adversary the devil

walks about like a roaring lion, seeking whom he may devour.

Since we are on earth and the devil is trying to devour us, it goes to say that he is on earth walking about. So the next time you hear someone refer to the devil in hell, you can point out the inaccuracy of what they are saying.

Another thing that can undermine our faith is the notion of self-forgiveness, a concept that is not supported by the Bible and is not real. Your shame and guilt following wrongdoing are not determined by your ability to forgive yourself; righteousness cannot be achieved through any actions or deeds.

We do not have the authority to forgive ourselves. If we could forgive ourselves, why would we need to confess our sins to God?

1 John 1:9 (NKJV) says:

If we confess our sins, He is faithful and just to forgive us our sins and to cleanse us from all unrighteousness.

If you believe that, then there is nothing more you need to do. Some people don't even feel remorse about their offenses and just keep going. If it were up to us to forgive ourselves, a lot would not. Let me bring your attention to the event in Mark 2:1-8. I would like you to zero in on what the scribes were thinking:

Who can forgive sins but God alone?

The scribes were correct; their problem was that they did not know Jesus was God in the flesh. Only God and God alone can forgive sins. We need to pay attention to what we say and believe, not just because somebody said it and it sounds biblical. With that said, it is not a free ticket to go around doing wrong because if you are truly a doer of the word, willfully offending others would not be a part of your new nature.

I would like to leave you with the following information when it comes to words. While Jesus was walking on earth, he used his words in some ways that made people wonder about his sanity. Jesus went around talking to trees, the sea, the wind, fever, and even dead people. In all of these instances, you can see how powerful words are. Use yours wisely!

If you think Jesus talked about these things because he is God, you are not wrong, but you are not entirely correct, either. In Mark 11:23 (NKJV), Jesus told us if we say:

For assuredly, I say to you, whoever says to this mountain, 'Be removed and be cast into the sea,' and does not doubt in his heart, but believes that those things he says will be done, he will have whatever he says.

As clear as day, you can see Jesus is saying we can do the same, but we must have faith in what you say.

I want to clarify that the intention behind this book is purely to provide knowledge and awareness with no judgment or criticism. I simply want to bring attention to our weaknesses, renew our minds, and embrace a mindset of faith.

About the Author

Bruno D. Cameron originally hails from Jamaica, where he spent the first 29 years of his life before relocating to America. He served in the U.S. Navy for 22 years, which allowed him to experience various cultures, spiritual beliefs, and religions. This exposure helped him see how people perceive God in different parts of the world.

The teachings of the Bible have always played a significant role in his life, greatly influencing his decision to write this book. His critical thinking and truth-seeking mindset have driven him to explore the answers a young believer needs to walk confidently by faith.

Bruno is married to Apostle Dr. Dana Cameron, the pastor of Life Changing Ministry in Suffolk,

Virginia. Together, they are proud parents of five wonderful children: Olivia Cameron, Abigail Cameron, Jeremiah Peprah, David Peprah, and Michael Cameron. "The Meaning of Life and Faith" is his first book.

www.ingramcontent.com/pod-product-compliance
Lightning Source LLC
Chambersburg PA
CBHW051212120626
46547CB00013B/1312